OSPREY AIRCRAFT OF THE ACES® • 79

Bristol F 2 Fighter Aces of World War 1

SERIES EDITOR: TONY HOLMES

OSPREY AIRCRAFT OF THE ACES® • 79

Bristol F 2 Fighter Aces of World War 1

Jon Guttman

OSPREY PUBLISHING

This book is dedicated to the memory of W F J Harvey and all the other 'Biff Boys'

First published in Great Britain in 2007 by Osprey Publishing
Midland House, West Way, Botley, Oxford, OX2 0PH
443 Park Avenue South, New York, NY, 10016, USA
E-mail; info@ospreypublishing.com

ISBN 13: 978 1 84603 201 1

Edited by Tony Holmes
Page design by Tony Truscott
Cover Artwork by Mark Postlethwaite
Aircraft Profiles by Harry Dempsey
Scale Drawings by Mark Styling
Index by Alan Thatcher
Originated by PDQ Digital Media Solutions
Printed and bound in China

07 08 09 10 11 10 9 8 7 6 5 4 3 2 1

For a catalogue of all books published by Osprey please contact:
NORTH AMERICA
Osprey Direct, C/o Random House Distribution Center,
400 Hahn Road, Westminster, MD 21157
E-mail:info@ospreydirect.com

ALL OTHER REGIONS
Osprey Direct UK, PO Box 140 Wellingborough, Northants, NN8 2FA, UK
E-mail: info@ospreydirect.co.uk
www.ospreypublishing.com

ACKNOWLEDGEMENTS
Thanks to Jack Eder, Norman Franks, Colin Huston, Philip Jarrett, Colin Owers, Charles Schaedel and Greg VanWyngarden, as well as the late Sir Victor E Groom, Stanley L Walters and William McKenzie Thomson.

Front cover
On 13 March 1918, Bristol F 2B C4630, crewed by Capt Geoffrey F Hughes and Lt Hugh Claye, led 11 aircraft of No 62 Sqn on an offensive patrol southeast of Cambrai at 16,000 ft. Spotting ten Fokker Dr I triplanes and ten Albatros D Vs 6000 ft below him, Hughes deliberately turned his flight so as to draw the enemy away from DH 4 bombers in the vicinity – he also gained the attention of five more Dr Is and five Pfalz D IIIs in the process.

'It was now five minutes after the time our patrol was due to land, and having succeeded in drawing all the enemy aircraft to a point just east of Cambrai, I considered our work was done and turned for the lines, not intending to be drawn into combat against at least 40 enemy aircraft', Hughes subsequently reported. 'As I turned to cross the lines I saw one of my Bristols dive on the triplanes below us. Apparently another machine thought that it was I who had dived, for he followed the first. This blunder upset all my plans, and I was forced to attack'.

After driving a Dr I off a Bristol's tail, Hughes fired 80 rounds into a second triplane that was threatening another of his squadronmates, apparently hitting the German pilot and sending the Fokker down out of control. Hughes then zoomed up to attack a red-nosed triplane, into which his observer, Claye, fired 50 rounds at 50 yards' distance until it fell vertically with its upper wing falling away in pieces.

In all, No 62 Sqn claimed six victories in the melée – two Dr Is to Hughes and Claye, a Dr I and an Albatros credited to Capt William E Staton and his observer, Lt Horace E Merritt (in C4619), an Albatros to 2Lt S W Symonds and Sgt W N Holmes, and an Albatros to Lts A R James and John Mathew Hay. The squadron lost two F 2Bs, however, with 2Lt Cyrus Allen being killed and 2Lt A B Will and Lts G R Crammond and N T Watson taken prisoner.

The only two German claims against Bristols that day were by Ltns Rudolf Heins and Franz Schleiff of *Jasta* 56, at the cost of Ltn d R Walter Bowein killed in action. Another German casualty was Ltn Lothar von Richthofen of *Jasta* 11, wounded when the wing of his red and yellow Dr I was shot up and he was badly injured in the ensuing crash landing. Manfred von Richthofen's younger brother was possibly the victim of either the team of Hughes and Claye, or Sopwith Camel pilot Capt Augustus H Orlebar of No 73 Sqn – who claimed a triplane southeast of Cambrai at the same time – or both (*Cover artwork by Mark Postlethwaite*)

CONTENTS

A STING IN THE TAIL

'A curious feature of the types of British aircraft of 1914-1918 was their marked individuality (like so many of those who flew them)', wrote Maj W F J Harvey, president of the Cross & Cockade Society of Great Britain and 26-victory ace of World War 1. 'Some were hated, some, like the pretty kittenish Sopwith Pup, were loved, some, like the SE 5 and the old workhorse FE 2b, were respected for their sterling qualities. The Farmans were funny jokes, one or two others were jokes in rather poor taste, and there was the Camel, that fantastic brainchild of Sopwith, which was both feared and respected. There was only one which was both respected and loved by all who flew it – the Bristol Fighter'.

The Bristol Fighter's genesis began in 1916, when the Royal Flying Corps (RFC) began seeking a reconnaissance aeroplane to replace the all-too-stable and painfully vulnerable BE 2c. The Royal Aircraft Factory, which created the BE, responded with the RE 8, whose principal improvement was to exchange the pilot's and observer's positions, giving the latter a vastly improved field of fire for his Scarff ring-mounted 0.303-in Lewis machine gun than he had had sitting amid the wings, struts and wires of the BE2c.

Meanwhile, at British Aeroplane Ltd in Bristol, its chief engineer, Frank Sowter Barnwell, also offered a replacement in the form of the R 2A, which featured a fuselage raised above the lower wing by struts in order to improve the pilot's view over the upper wing. A revised version of the Bristol design with unequal-span wings and a 150-hp V8 Hispano-Suiza engine was designated the R 2B, but it was quickly superseded by another variant with equal-span wings and a new 190-hp Rolls-Royce Falcon I V12 engine.

At that point, Barnwell's brainchild was being regarded as a 'reconnaissance-fighter', and by the time the first prototype (A3303) flew on 9 September 1916, it had been redesignated as the F 2A. With its side-mounted 'ear' radiators replaced by a circular radiator in the nose, A3303 underwent its official tests between 16 and 18 October, using both a two and four-bladed propeller. The RFC was already impressed with the new aeroplane's potential, and testing only confirmed its decision to order 50 production examples.

It might be noted at this point that the term 'fighter' was used more often for two-seat than single-seat aircraft. The latter were originally short-range reconnaissance aeroplanes appropriately called 'scouts', and after they were successfully armed with machine guns, the RFC continued to use that term for them throughout the war. Other nations, however, referred to single-seaters by such reflections on their lone hunter status as the French *'avion de chasse'*, the German *'Jagdflugzeug'*

Capt William Leefe Robinson, who had been awarded the Victoria Cross for destroying Schütte-Lanz airship SL-11 over north London on the night of 2-3 September 1916, was the most famous of No 48 Sqn's flight commanders, but tragically mishandled the Bristol F 2As he led on their first combat mission on 5 April 1917 (*Raymond L Rimell*)

and American 'pursuit plane'. A fighter, on the other hand, was essentially a reconnaissance aeroplane with either the armament or performance to take care of itself, the most notable previous example being the Royal Aircraft Factory's 'Farman Experimental' FE 2 – a large, lumbering two-seat pusher that, thanks to tactics devised by its crews, had proven to be surprisingly difficult prey to its attackers.

The first operational F 2As were delivered to No 48 Sqn in December 1916, armed with a synchronised 0.303-in Vickers gun forward and a Lewis gun flexibly mounted on a Scarff ring in the observer's pit. After training at Rendcombe, in Gloucestershire, the unit was deployed to Bellevue, in France, in March 1917, its aeroplanes being held until the start of the Battle of Arras in the hope of their achieving a degree of surprise over the enemy. Perhaps not coincidentally, the first of the Royal Aircraft Factory's latest 'Scout Experimentals' (better known as the SE 5) was also to make its combat debut at that time, with No 56 Sqn.

As with No 56 Sqn's SE 5s (see *Osprey Aircraft of the Aces 78 – SE 5/5a Aces of World War 1* for further details), the Bristol crews of No 48 Sqn were led by a cadre of veteran flight and deputy flight leaders. Capt Arthur T Cull had seen considerable action, and the Oxford-educated Capt Alan Machin Wilkinson, born in Eastbourne, Sussex, on 21 November 1891, had previously served in the Hampshire Regiment of the Territorial Force and then scored ten victories flying DH 2s with No 24 Sqn before joining No 48 Sqn on 16 January 1917. Finally, Capt William Leefe Robinson, who had been awarded the Victoria Cross for destroying Schütte-Lanz airship SL-11 over north London on the night of 2-3 September 1916, was the unit's most famous flight commander, but he had only secondary knowledge of the more intense combat environment that had developed over the Western Front when he flew his first mission in April 1917.

OFFENSIVES

Seen in the larger perspective of World War 1, April 1917 was the month in which French General Robert Nivelle launched the great offensive that became known as the Second Battle of the Aisne – begun rather belatedly on the 16th, and destined to end in bloody disappointment. The British offensive, intended to support Nivelle's, actually occurred one week earlier, on 9 April, and succeeded at least in taking Vimy Ridge. Amid the casualty reports that flooded the Allied headquarters came a bit of promising news for the future – the United States had declared war against Germany on 6 April.

While such significant events transpired on earth, the skies above the Western Front saw a prodigious burst of aerial activity as the RFC, the Royal Naval Air Service (RNAS) and the *Aviation Française* flew in support of the ground offensives, only to suffer disproportionate losses to the waiting German fighter squadrons, known as *Jagdstaffeln* or *Jastas*. Amid that aerial slaughter, the month that went down in British aviation history as 'Bloody April' saw the debuts of both the SE 5 and the F 2A.

As fortune would have it, Capt Robinson was slated to lead the first offensive patrol by No 48 Sqn's Bristols, over Douai. Much has been made of the disaster that followed, but it was very much a unique circumstance. Ignoring the higher speed and greater manoeuvrability that the F 2A offered over other Allied two-seaters, Robinson adhered to the standard tactic of closing up the flight when attacked so that the rear gunners could provide each other with mutual support. He also disregarded advice not to fly at the low altitude of 4000 ft.

'Robinson did not appreciate the fact that the Bristol could be used as an offensive weapon by the pilot, and that it was not necessary to provide one another with protection', recounted squadronmate Capt Wilkinson after the event. 'We were not bothered about Robinson's VC – only that he seemed to dislike any opinion other than his own in matters of which, I might say, he had no experience'.

On top of that, Robinson reportedly learned that the lubricating oil in the machine guns froze at high altitude. His solution was to tell the gunnery officer, 'If the guns are freezing up through the freezing of the oil, stop oiling the guns, and therefore there will be nothing to freeze'.

With the benefit of hindsight, Robinson was in woefully over his head. VC or not, he was entering a combat environment completely different from Zeppelin hunting in home defence as he led his six-aeroplane flight up at 1000 hrs on 5 April.

By the time the Bristols neared Arras at 1100 hrs, German ground observers had reported their presence to the fighter unit at Brayelle, and soon five Albatros D IIIs of *Jasta* 11 were taking off to intercept them. In contrast to Robinson, the German commander, Oblt Manfred *Freiherr* von Richthofen, had served his apprenticeship in *Jasta* 2 under the father of tactical fighter doctrine, Hptm Oswald Boelcke, before taking command of *Jasta* 11 in January 1917 and turning it into the deadliest outfit in the *Luftstreitkräfte*. By April 5, von Richthofen had 34 Allied aeroplanes to his credit and his all-red Albatros D III was becoming a familiar and feared sight over the Western Front.

The same could also be said for the Red Baron's 'gentlemen' in *Jasta* 11, several of whom also boasted scores that would have rated them as 'aces' with five or more victories had the Germans recognised the Allied term at the time.

As the Germans closed in on the formation, Robinson's Bristols closed up, their gunners waiting for the enemy to come within range. The Albatros scouts bore in fast, twin machine guns blazing, and almost immediately F 2A A3340 fell out of formation and was forced down near Lewaarde by von Richthofen himself. Its crew was wounded, but the pilot, 2Lt Arthur N Lechler, managed to set fire to his

The burnt remains of Bristol F 2A A3340 of No 48 Sqn after it was brought down at Lewaarde, southeast of Douai, by *Jasta* 11's leader, Hptm Manfred *Freiherr* von Richthofen, on 5 April 1917. Although both crewmen were wounded, the pilot, 2Lt A N Lechler, managed to set the aeroplane on fire before being taken prisoner. His observer, Lt H D K George, died of his wounds on 23 May (*Norman Franks*)

Bristol F 2A A3343 was also brought down on 5 April 1917 by Manfred von Richthofen, its crew, Lts H T Adams and D J Stewart of No 48 Sqn, force-landing their aircraft near Cuincy. Both men were duly taken prisoner (*Norman Franks*)

aeroplane with his Very pistol before being taken prisoner. His observer, 2Lt Herbert D K George, succumbed to his wounds in the Douai hospital shortly afterwards.

While von Richthofen climbed to rejoin the chase, the Bristol gunners did their best to engage their darting assailants, only to find their weapons, left unlubricated at Robinson's orders, seizing up and falling silent. Vzfw Sebastian Festner drove down Robinson and his observer, New Zealander 2Lt Edward D Warburton, both of whom became Prisoners of War (PoWs). Eventually catching up with Bristol A3343 near Cuincy, von Richthofen downed Lts H T Adams and D J Stewart, who were also wounded and taken prisoner. A fourth Bristol was brought down by Ltn Georg Simon for his first victory, resulting in another wounded aircrew, Lt Horace A Cooper and 2Lt A Boldison, falling into German captivity.

The remaining two F 2As limped home full of holes. One was crewed by Lt P Pike and 2Lt Hugh Bradford Griffith. The latter was the 24-year-old son of a doctor from Montreal, Canada, who had been an art student at McGill University when war broke out in 1914, and who, after a year in No 6 Canadian Field Ambulance, joined the RFC in October 1916. Griffith had been an observer in FE 2bs and FE 2ds with Nos 20 and 11 Sqns prior to transferring to No 48 Sqn on 17 March 1917.

Upon returning to his airfield, Griffith reported that his aeroplane had become separated from the formation during the combat, and in a lone rearguard action he had driven down an assailant at 1050 hrs. He also stated that he saw a Bristol diving down trailing smoke, and three others heavily engaged by a superior number of enemy fighters. Griffith saw one of the German fighters driven down out of control by Robinson and Warburton. These two claims were officially credited as No 48 Sqn's first victories, but the sad truth was summed up by von Richthofen;

'After the attack, which was similar to a cavalry charge, the enemy squadron lay demolished on the ground. Not a single one of us was even wounded.'

It is one of the earliest ironies of military aviation – although by no means the last – that one of history's most successful combat aircraft could have started its fighting career on so inauspicious a note. But while von Richthofen had reasonable cause to dismiss the new two-seater, it must be noted that he and his seasoned paladins had been aided by an enemy flight leader who had done things just about as wrongly as he possibly could.

Later in the F 2A's disastrous first day of combat on 5 April 1917, Capt Alan Machin Wilkinson demonstrated what the Bristol could do if used more aggressively. As a flight leader in No 48 Sqn, he added nine victories to the previous ten he had scored in DH 2s with No 24 Sqn (*Norman Franks*)

A Canadian born in Australia, early F 2A exponent Fred Parkinson Holliday scored his first victory on 6 April 1917 and had increased his tally to 17 by 27 July. He finished the war with the rank of major (*Norman Franks*)

More Losses

The Bristol's 'black day' was far from over, as a second patrol, aggressively led by Capt Wilkinson, encountered three Albatros near Douai, two of which Wilkinson and his 24-year-old observer Lt Laurence William Allen from Coventry drove down. The patrol claimed another enemy 'driven down' before it returned safely.

While leading the day's third patrol, Irish-born Capt David Mary Tidmarsh, a former infantryman who had scored three victories in DH 2s with No 24 Sqn prior to joining No 48 Sqn, engaged a two-seater east of Douai, only to see it escape into the clouds. 2Lt Oswald W Berry attacked another enemy aeroplane southeast of Douai and drove it down in a steep spiral, while Lt George N Brockhurst engaged and drove down a red scout. Only Wilkinson's and Allen's victory was credited as 'out of control', but those second and third sorties did much to restore No 48 Sqn's shaken confidence in its new machines.

In the days that followed, the unit's aircrews became better acquainted with their aeroplanes, and learned to take advantage of the F 2A's speed and manoeuvrability – brisker than the average two-seater – by using it as one would a single-seat scout, with the added asset of a 'sting in the tail'.

Two Bristol crews claimed enemy aeroplanes 'out of control' northeast of Arras on 6 April, with one victim possibly being Uffz Ludwig Weber of *Jasta* 3, who was wounded. One of these victories was the first for the team of Capts Fred Parkinson Holliday and Anthony Herbert William Wall.

Born in Melbourne, in the Australian state of Victoria, on 20 February 1888, Holliday was educated in England and was working for the Swedish General Electric Company in Canada when war broke out. Later serving as a sapper in the 2nd Field Company, Royal Canadian Engineers, he survived a chlorine gas attack in 1915. Holliday served as an observer in No 4 Sqn from December 1915 to August 1916, then trained to be a pilot. His 28-year-old observer, Wall, was a Londoner who had been an extensively travelled journalist for the *Daily Mail* before the war, later serving in the Belgian army and the 17th Battalion of the Middlesex Regiment, before transferring to the RFC as an observer.

The first time the Germans acknowledged a serious loss to the Bristols occurred on 8 April, when a flight of F 2As flying an offensive patrol between Arras, Lens and Vitry were attacked by Albatros D IIIs of *Jasta* 4. Skilful mutual support resulted in claims for six Germans driven down, of which one was later credited as 'out of control' to Capt Tidmarsh and 2Lt C B Holland and 2Lts Oswald W Berry and F B Goodison, while a second was awarded to the teams of 2Lts George Brockhurst and C B Boughton, Robert E Adeney and Leslie G Lovell, and A J Riley and L G Hall.

This time, one of the unit's claims was genuine, inflicting a demoralising loss on the enemy. D III 1958/16 broke up before crashing between Vitry and Sailly, killing *Jasta* 4's commander, Ltn Wilhelm Frankl, a recipient of the *Orden Pour le Mérite* who had just scored his 20th victory the day before. Frankl's demise, however, may well have been caused, or at least abetted, by structural failure of his D III's sesquiplane lower wing – a problem that had been plaguing the otherwise superb Albatros since its debut in late January (see *Osprey*

F 2A A3319 displays typical markings adopted by No 48 Sqn by the end of April 1917 – namely flight colours on the wheel hubs and white numerals on the fuselage side and upper decking. A3319 was withdrawn for training duties at Rendcombe on 27 July 1917 and was written off in a crash on 30 August (*Colin A Owers*)

Aircraft of the Aces 32 – Albatros Aces of World War 1 and *Osprey Aircraft of the Aces 77 – Albatros Aces of World War 1 Part Two* for further details). Nevertheless, any celebrating at No 48 Sqn that evening would be muted at best, for as the patrol continued, it was attacked east of Arras by more Albatros, this time from *Jasta* Boelcke. Ltn Otto Bernert forced F 2A A3330 down near Remy with Berry dead – his observer, Goodison, died of his wounds on 26 May.

Patrolling continued without let-up, with the team of Wilkinson and Griffith having shares in three Albatros D IIIs and a two-seater on 9 April, for which Wilkinson would be awarded a Bar to his Distinguished Service Order (DSO) on 25 May. Tidmarsh and Holland and Brockhurst and Boughton shared in another victory on 10 April, and on the 11th Tidmarsh was leading three other F 2As on patrol when *Jasta* 11 dived on them over Fampoux at 0830 hrs. Tidmarsh, Holland, Brockhurst, Broughton, Adeney, Lovell, Riley and Hall were jointly credited with two Albatros D IIIs in the ensuing fight, but again *Jasta* 11 recorded no losses, while taking a painful toll on No 48 Sqn for the second time in a week.

Adeney and Lovell were killed by Ltn Karl Emil Schäfer, while Brockhurst and Boughton were killed by Ltn Lothar von Richthofen, this being his second victory since joining his older brother's *Staffel* – and by no means his last over Bristols. Tidmarsh and Holland were more fortunate, being brought down alive by Ltn Kurt Wolff, but they spent the rest of the war as PoWs, leaving only Wilkinson from No 48 Sqn's starting line-up of veteran flight leaders.

Wilkinson and Allen teamed up with 2Lts William Otto Braasch Winkler and Ernest S Moore to down an Albatros on 12 April. Wilkinson was leading a line patrol on Friday the 13th when his flight was attacked by about 20 enemy fighters near Vitry-en-Artois. One was credited as destroyed by Wilkinson and Allen, and a second as 'out of control' to 2Lts J W Warren and Hugh Griffith. On the way home, however, 2Lts H D Davies and R S Worsley were brought down by flak near Courcelles and taken prisoner.

Wilkinson and Allen sent an Albatros down out of control on the 22nd for the former's last victory before being transferred to command No 23 Sqn, which was equipped with SPAD VIIs. Administrative tasks would prevent Wilkinson from further flying, or scoring, but he had done much to show what the Bristol Fighter could do, and how to do it. Griffith, now an observer ace, was subsequently promoted to captain, and instructed in Britain, Canada and the United States. After the war he sold life insurance, before eventually passing away in April 1974.

At the end of May 1917, No 11 Sqn began replacing its FE 2bs with F 2As to become the second operational Bristol Fighter unit, although it only had five aircraft when it joined No 48 Sqn at La Bellevue on 1 June. By then, too, the first F 2Bs had arrived to replace No 48 Sqn's depleted ranks, from which several war-weary F 2As were consequently handed down to No 11 Sqn.

IMPROVED F 2B

In spite of their disastrous initial showing, another 200 Bristol Fighters were ordered for the RFC, modified with longer-span tailplanes and a slope to the upper fuselage longerons that somewhat improved the pilot's forward and downward visibility. The first 150 F 2Bs, as the altered Bristols were officially designated, used Hispano-Suiza engines, but the next 50 were powered by the 220 hp Rolls-Royce Falcon II, with radiator shutters to help control the engine's temperature. Aircraft production was handicapped by engine availability, but while later F 2Bs would be tested with other motors, including the Siddeley Puma, the 200 hp Sunbeam Arab and the 400 hp Liberty, none achieved the balance of airframe and powerplant that made the Falcon-engined F 2B such a success.

The F 2B had a wingspan of 39 ft, 3 in, was 25 ft 10 in long and had a height of 9 ft 9 in. Its empty weight was 2145 lb and maximum take-off weight was 3243 lb. The aeroplane boasted a maximum speed of 123 mph at 5000 ft, and it climbed at an average rate of 889 ft per minute to a service ceiling of 18,000 ft and a maximum ceiling of 21,500 ft. Armament originally consisted of a single synchronised forward-firing Vickers machine gun and a Scarff ring-mounted Lewis for the observer, as well as up to 240 lb of either 20-lb Cooper or 112-lb Hale bombs. In the field, Bristol crews often augmented their firepower with a second Lewis on the Scarff ring or on a forward-firing mounting above the upper wing.

The F 2B's combat debut on 2 May 1917 reflected the improved tactics that No 48 Sqn had already introduced with its F 2As. The day began at 1000 hrs when 2Lts H C Furnes and H Davis (in F 2A A3349) and Lts Thomas Percy Middleton and Charles G Claye (in A3325) drove an Albatros two-seater down out of control east of Adinfer Wood – the second victory for the latter team, which had previously downed an Albatros D III on 30 April.

During an evening patrol, the Bristols got into a running fight over Brebières, Biache and Vitry, during which Winkler and Moore claimed three Albatros D IIIs, and two more were credited to Lt Owen F J Scholte and 2nd Air Mechanic (2AM) F W Dames. In addition, 2Lts L G Harrison and H L E Richards sent an Albatros down out of control, although they were both wounded in the action, and Capt Cull and 1AM Arthur Trusson drew first blood for the F 2B (A7101) with an Albatros D III out of control.

The F 2Bs began adding steadily to No 48 Sqn's rising account after that, particularly the seasoned team of Holliday and Wall in A7108, who downed a two-seater and three Albatros D IIIs on 9 May, and two more D IIIs during an offensive patrol on the 11th. The latter action brought the first F 2B losses, however, again at the deadly hands of *Jasta* 11. A7101 – the first F 2B to arrive at No 48 Sqn, and the first to score – was also the first destroyed, as Ltn Wilhelm Allmenröder despatched it in flames east of Arras, killing Cull and Trusson.

Five minutes later, A7111 was brought down at Gavrelle by Lothar von Richthofen – its pilot, Lt W O B Winkler, whose score then stood at six, was killed, while 2Lt Ernest S Moore, who had seven victories to his credit, was taken prisoner.

A former Royal Engineer and pilot in Nos 18 and 51 (Home Defence) Sqns, Lt Owen John Frederick Scholte from Hampstead, in London, was credited with two Albatros D IIIs – one in flames – flying F 2A A3347, with 2AM F W Dames as his observer, on 2 May 1917. He scored four more victories in F 2Bs and had been awarded the MC by 5 September. Scholte added a further pair of victories to his tally in SE 5as as a flight leader in No 60 Sqn on 15 and 19 May 1918, but was subsequently killed in a motor accident on 30 July (*Norman Franks*)

On 17 May the squadron got a new flight commander in the person of Capt Richard Raymond-Barker. Born on 6 May 1894, commissioned on 30 November 1914 and transferred to the RFC on 6 August 1915, Raymond-Barker had qualifed as a pilot in October, and after being posted to France on 22 November, had flown BEs with Nos 6 and 16 Sqns until 26 December 1916.

Flying F 2B A7112, the veteran Raymond-Barker showed his mettle during an escort on 20 May, which led to several engagements against superior numbers of enemy machines. In one, Lt H M Fraser and Pvte J H Muscott downed an adversary, while Raymond-Barker and his observer, Pvte Robert N W Jeff, sent an Albatros D III down out of control over Brebières and shared another with 2Lts H J Pratt and H Owen. Six days later, Raymond-Barker and Jeff destroyed a D III east of Brebières, and on 5 June Raymond-Barker and Sgt Nicholson downed a two-seater.

Transferred to No 11 Sqn on 2 July, Raymond-Barker quickly added two more to his score – an Albatros D V on the 8th, with Pvte Jack Mason as his observer (Mason would go on to score four more in concert with 9-victory ace Lt Ronald Frank Strickland Mauduit) and a D III with 2Lt E J Price on the 17th. In September, Raymond-Barker was promoted to major and given command of No 3 Sqn, which required the radical transition from the tractable Bristol to the tricky single-seat Sopwith Camel. Raymond-Barker added no further victories to his score, but earned the dubious distinction of dying in flames on 20 April 1918 as the 79th, and penultimate, victim of Manfred von Richthofen.

Future Kiwi Ace

On 7 July 1917, No 48 Sqn acquired a less-than-promising replacement from New Zealand. Born in Thames, near Auckland, on 15 June 1890, Keith Rodney Park had served in Egypt and Gallipoli with the New Zealand Artillery, before receiving a commission in July 1915 and switching to the Royal Artillery on 3 September. He served with the 29th Division in France until 21 October 1916, when an exploding shell threw him from his horse. The resulting back injury led to Park being pronounced fit only for home service. He would have none of that, however, and when he discovered that his medical records had been lost somewhere between a French field hospital and Woolwich Arsenal, where he had been assigned as an artillery instructor, he wangled his way into the RFC, where his initial work as a flight instructor allowed him to accumulate 100 flying hours by the time he joined No 48 Sqn.

Park's first observer, 2Lt Arthur Rex Hurden Noss, was from Crouch End, in north London, and had previously scored two victories with Lt H M Fraser as his pilot, on 27 May and 11 June. Park's luck still seemed to run sour, however, as magneto problems during a patrol

Lt Keith Rodney Park stands at left beside No 48 Sqn F 2B A7274 in September 1917 (*Jack Eder*)

One of No 48 Sqn's early F 2Bs, A7220 is shown in the unit markings officially authorised by 26 August 1917. On that day 2Lt James A W Binnie and Cpl V Reed destroyed a two-seater and drove an Albatros D V down out of control. On 11 September Binnie was flying A7220 with Lt Thomas C S Tuffield as his observer when they downed a DFW C V out of control near Dixmuide (*Philip Jarrett*)

on 19 July led to a forced landing that badly damaged F 2B A7118 and injured Noss. During a photo-reconnaissance with 2Lt A W Merchant on the 24th, Park was attacked by three Albatros D IIIs, but Merchant coolly fired into one at 200 yards and drove it down in a vertical nose dive, to be credited to Park and himself as out of control, while the other two attackers retired.

On 12 August, Park, reunited with Noss, downed an Albatros D III out of control, and they repeated the performance on a DFW C V on the 16th. During a morning patrol in Bristol A7182 on the 17th, Park and Noss noticed eight Albatros D IIIs at about 0655 hrs, and when three dived on a Sopwith Camel, Park went after them and drove them off, only to be attacked from behind by two more. Noss engaged those assailants, and when they overshot, Park let them have it with his Vickers, causing one to fall out of control and another to crash west of Slype. Three more fighters pounced on the Bristol, but Noss sent one spinning down out of control. As Park pursued it, three more Albatros dived on him, but again overshot. Park then saw a Camel with an enemy aeroplane on its tail, and closed to 50 yards range before firing 100 rounds into the German and seeing it fall into a spin.

Born in Glasgow on 25 June 1894, 2Lt James Alexander Weatherhead Binnie survived the war with nine victories to his name, while his usual observer, Cpl V Reed, was credited with six (*Norman Franks*)

Both Park and Noss were gazetted for the Military Cross (MC) for their quadruple victory, but in the same action, 2Lt H F Gough's Bristol was attacked, his engine hit and his observer, Capt Leopold F Reincke, mortally wounded, although Gough managed to get his aeroplane home. During another patrol later that morning, three of the squadron's Bristols were attacked by an identical number of Albatros at 1100 hrs, but the combined fire of 2Lt L H Tanner and Lt James Bruce Jameson, the respective observers of 2Lt Alan Craddock Simpson's and Capt John Herbert Towne Letts' F 2Bs, resulted in one German spinning down under full power and then falling to pieces in the air, probably accounting for the death of Ltn Franz Götte of *Jasta* 20.

On 21 August Park was flying a patrol at 13,000 ft with 2Lt William O'Toole, another veteran observer from Sutton, Surrey, with four victories already to his credit, when they spotted six Albatros D Vs and dived on them. They failed to achieve results, but as they were climbing back to rejoin the formation, eight more Albatros attacked them. Again closely teaming up, Park and O'Toole sent one antagonist down out of control and then, as two others overshot in their attack on O'Toole, Park shot another down with his forward gun. More Germans got on the Bristol's tail and disabled O'Toole's Lewis gun, but Park dived and finally managed to elude them.

One of the early F 2Bs to arrive at No 48 Sqn, A7107 was used by Lt Ralph L Curtis and 2Lt Laurence W Allen to destroy an Albatros D III for Curtis' first and Allen's 10th, and final, victory on 16 June 1917. Curtis flew it again with his usual observer, 2Lt Desmond P F Uniacke, when they destroyed an Albatros D V over Vitry on 7 July. On 21 July, Lt Brian E Baker and 2Lt G R Spencer drove down a D V out of control over Slype for the second of Baker's 12 credited victories. A7107 is shown here after it had returned to the UK for Home Establishment training duties (*Colin A Owers*)

Born in Finchley, London, on 31 July 1891, Lt Alan Douglas Light was credited with eight victories as an observer in No 48 Sqn. After suffering a concussion and a head wound in a crash on 11 September 1917, he became an airship pilot, escorting North Sea convoys in non-rigid airship NS8. After a career as a rubber planter in Malaya, he served as an air gunner with Coastal Command's No 209 Sqn during World War 2 (*Jack Eder*)

O'Toole downed a third D V later that afternoon while flying with Capt John Theobald Milne as his pilot, and on the 25th Milne and O'Toole claimed a D V out of control – the latter's eighth success before being posted home on 6 September – while Park and Noss claimed a D V in flames in the same action.

On 2 September Park accounted for two more Albatros D Vs with 2Lt Alan Douglas Light as his observer. Three days later, Park and 2AM H Lindfield were attacked by three D Vs, one of which overshot, at which point Park fired five bursts into it and saw it crash into the sea four miles north of Ostend. Nearby, Lt Ralph Luxmore Curtis and 2Lt H Munro shot an Albatros D V down in flames off Westende, their victim probably being Ltn Franz Pernet of *Jasta* Boelcke, stepson of General Erich Ludendorff.

On 11 September Park was made a flight commander, having also been awarded a Bar to his MC and the French *Croix de Guerre*. On the 14th he was leading an evening patrol with 2Lt Hugh Owen, a former actor from Wheathampstead, Hertfordshire, as his observer, when they spotted ten Albatros D Vs below and dived on them. As was becoming the norm, Owen fired a drum of Lewis at an attacker, then Park pursued it, firing 150 rounds at 100 yards' range until it fell out of control. Seeing another Albatros attacking his patrol, Park intervened, and when it disengaged, followed firing until he saw the pilot slump forward in his seat and the fighter burst into flames, to crash south of Dixmuide. Its pilot, Ltn Maximillian von Chelius of *Jasta* Boelcke, was killed.

His inauspicious beginning notwithstanding, Park's score now stood at 16, but on 15 September 2Lt E B Corry crashed while landing F 2B A7217, and his observer, Noss – whose personal tally then stood at nine, seven of which he'd scored with Park – died of his injuries the next day.

Lt Ralph Luxmore Curtis was credited with 13 victories between 16 June and 17 September 1917, his victims including an Albatros D V in flames off Westende on 5 September – this aircraft was probably flown by General Erich Ludendorff's godson, Ltn Franz Pernet of *Jasta* Boelcke. Curtis was himself killed on 21 September by Ltn Hermann Göring of *Jasta* 27 (*Norman Franks*)

Park had no more successes for the rest of the year, but he was promoted to captain and was lucky to survive his Bristol being set afire by anti-aircraft fire over enemy territory. Managing to glide back over the lines, he later recalled, 'If your aeroplane was on fire, you immediately switched off your petrol supply and opened wide the throttle to use up the fuel. Then you flung your aeroplane into a vertical sideslip, so that the flames roared away from your exposed head and shoulders. After that, you just prayed that the fire would burn itself out, and that you could pull your aeroplane out of that sideways dive'.

The son of Grimsby Alderman W S Beales, Sgt Walter Beales was credited with nine enemy aeroplanes destroyed. He survived being shot up on 23 March – when he and Capt William Lewis Wells scored three victories – a hand wound five days later and being brought down in Allied lines by a pilot of *Jasta* 46 on 9 May after he and Capt Charles George Douglas Napier had accounted for three enemy scouts (*Norman Franks*)

During a fight with six Albatros south of Dixmuide on 24 October, 2Lt H F Jenkins and 1AM E J Dunford claimed an opponent in flames and Jenkins brought his aeroplane back in spite of wounds to his left arm. However, the highly regarded Capt Milne, whose score then stood at nine, and his observer, 2Lt S Wright, were killed by Ltn Fritz Kieckhaefer of *Jasta* 29. Fellow flight commander Park performed the melancholy task of delivering Milne's effects to his wife in London – and in so doing was introduced to her cousin, Dorothy Margarita Parish. Soon after the war Park would marry Miss Parish, a happy union that would last nearly 53 years.

F 2B B1271 warms up for take-off at No 48 Sqn's aerodrome at Bertangles in April 1918. On 6 April 2Lt Vivian Voss and Lt Colin J R Gibson used this aeroplane to drive down a Fokker Dr I out of control south of Christ. Later serving in No 88 Sqn, Voss was eventually credited with four victories, but is better known for his memoir *Flying Minnows*, written under the pseudonym of 'Roger Vee' (*Jack Eder*)

Park and 2Lt John Henry Robertson were photographing the Bohain-St Quentin railway on 3 January 1918 when a DFW C V, aggressively piloted by future five-victory ace Uffz Kurt Ungewitter of *Schlachtstaffel* 5, attacked them. Park counterattacked, closing to 50 yards, and Robertson got in a good burst as the DFW passed under them, the latter then departing in a steep dive. As the Bristol team continued the mission it was attacked by six Albatros D IIIs, but Park and Robertson drove one of their antagonists down in a vertical dive, credited as out of control. The fight continued over Remicourt, with a German getting a burst into Park's motor, which began to

This photograph of a pipe-smoking Maj Keith Park was taken shortly after he had been made CO of No 48 Sqn in April 1918 (*Jack Eder*)

Maj Park poses before F 2B C814, in which Canadian-born Lt Robert H Little scored two of his six victories, but in which Park himself scored none. C814 was shot down near Proyart on 3 May 1918 by Offz Stv Paul Aue of *Jasta* 10, with pilot 2Lt A C G Brown dying of his injuries and gunner Cpl A W Sainsbury being wounded and taken prisoner (*Jack Eder*)

smoke and vibrate badly. Park went into a steep dive toward St Quentin and managed to outrun the three Albatros still giving chase, but at an altitude of 9000 ft his engine seized and again he had to glide his way to a forced landing on the Allied side of the lines.

Robertson's joint success with Park was only the first of five, the rest being scored with Lt Herbert Henry Hartley in F 2B A7114 – three Albatros D Vs on 8 March 1918 and a Fokker Dr I on the 11th. Robertson was hit in the latter action, however, and died of his wounds that same day. Hartley, for whom that triplane represented his seventh victory since September 1917, was shot through the heart during a fight over Estrées three days later, but his wounded observer, 2Lt G Dixon, managed to seize the controls and brought their Bristol (C4640) home for a landing.

Capt Leonard Allen Payne downed his first opponent with No 48 Sqn on 29 October 1917, became a flight commander in May 1918 and scored one of the unit's last three victories – his 11th – on 4 November (*Norman Franks*)

Promoted to major on 10 April, Park took over command of No 48 Sqn from Maj Horace Scott Shield MC, who had led the unit since 18 August 1917. In spite of his increased administrative duties, Park found time to shoot down a Pfalz D IIIa on 18 May, with 2Lt G J Maynard as his observer, and on 25 June he and 2Lt H Knowles destroyed a Rumpler and drove down a DFW out of control. That made Park, with 20, the top scorer in the squadron he led.

A former BE pilot in No 13 Sqn, Lt Brian Edmund Baker became a replacement flight leader in No 48 Sqn and scored 12 victories in F 2Bs, including a Gotha G IV bomber caught northwest of Ostend on 22 July 1917 as it was returning from a raid on England. Awarded the DSO and MC, he flew Bristols with No 141 (Home Defence) Sqn at Biggin Hill in 1918, served in World War 2 and retired as Air Marshal Sir Brian Baker. He eventually passed away on 8 October 1979, aged 83 (*Norman Franks*)

The pioneer Bristol Fighter unit claimed the last three of its 317 victories on 4 November 1918, with one (a Fokker D VII) being the 11th for Capt Leonard Allen Payne. After Park, the squadron's top-scorer was Maj Fred Holliday, all but the 17th of whose victories had been shared with Anthony Wall – that last, a DFW C V, had been driven down out of control on 27 July 1917 with the aid of 2Lt O'Toole. Moving to Sweden after the war, then returning to Canada in 1923, Holliday became president of Swedish Electric and rose to group captain rank in the Royal Canadian Air Force (RCAF) in World War 2. He died on 5 March 1980 at the ripe old age of 92.

Third among the 32 pilots who attained ace status in No 48 Sqn was 2Lt Ralph L Curtis from Braintree, in Essex, who scored all but two of his 15 victories with 2Lt Desmond Percival Fitzgerald Uniacke as his observer between 3 July and 17 September 1917. On the 21st, however, they were shot down near Roulers by Ltn Hermann Göring of *Jasta* 27, Curtis dying of his wounds and Uniacke being taken prisoner.

Capt John Letts, whose total came to 13, became a single-seat fighter pilot and a flight leader in No 64 Sqn in 1918. While taking off in an SE 5a of No 32 Sqn on 11 October, he suddenly went into a roll and crashed to his death.

Other 'leading lights' of No 48 Sqn included Capt Brian Edmund Baker with 12, and Capt Harold Anthony Oaks from Hespelar, Ontario, and Leonard Payne from Swaziland with 11 each. Nine of Alan Wilkinson's wartime total of 19 victories were scored while developing suitable fighting tactics for the Bristol, and Thomas Middleton claimed seven of his 28 victories with No 48 Sqn, the rest being scored with No 20 Sqn.

Among No 48 Sqn's 'lesser lights', Lt Robert Dodds, from Hamilton, Ontario, stood out for an action on 3 September 1917. He and 2Lt Thomas Cecil Silwood Tuffield, whose father was employed in Bombay, India, when he was born on 17 February 1893, were escorting DH 4 bombers of No 5 Sqn RNAS when their Bristol (A7222) came under attack by two Albatros north of Dixmuide at 0815 hrs.

One of No 48 Sqn's many observer aces, 2Lt Desmond Percival Fitzgerald Uniacke was credited with 13 victories before being brought down with Ralph Curtis by Ltn Hermann Göring on 21 September 1917. Uniacke was wounded during the engagement and taken prisoner (*Norman Franks*)

Canadian Bristol ace Lt Robert Dodds, who was born in Hamilton, Ontario, was credited with 10 or 11 enemy aeroplanes destroyed during his time with No 48 Sqn (*Jack Eder*)

A photograph from the marriage of Dorothy Margarita Woodbine-Parish and Maj Keith R Park almost two weeks after the armistice, on 25 November 1918. The union lasted 53 years, during which time No 48 Sqn's CO, and leading ace, would add further to his laurels in another world war (*Jack Eder*)

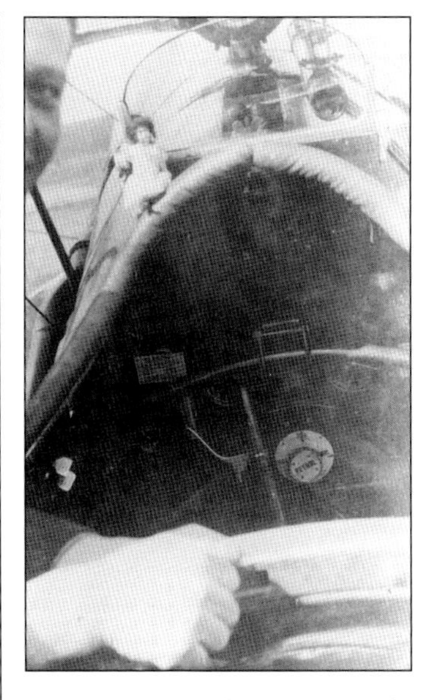

This photograph of the pilot's seat of 2Lt Herbert Thomas' No 48 Sqn F 2B, nicknamed *Enid*, was taken from the observer's position – note *Enid's* doll behind the windscreen! 'The Bowden lever on the left side of the joystick was hard to squeeze, and therefore you needed two hands to fire the Vickers gun', Thomas commented. The fuel gauge can be seen to the right of the control column (*Herbert Thomas via Jon Guttman*)

'While escorting DH 4s on bombing, we were attacked by two Albatros Scouts on our return', Dodds wrote in his combat report. 'The first machine attacked us, but I manoeuvred and got my front gun on him, and then he passed under my right wing, and my observer emptied a drum into him and drove him down, appearing out of control. The second one appeared immediately on our tail and above us – my observer fired into him at 200 yards range, and I turned and got between him and the sun, and we were head-on firing from a range of about 100 yards down to finally 25 yards, after which the enemy went down with flames issuing from his machine, which was completely out of control. My observer fired 150 rounds in the fight and myself 300'.

Dodds' and Tuffield's second claim (the fourth victory for both crewmen) turned out to be Hptm Otto Hartmann, commander of *Jasta* 28 and victor over seven Allied aeroplanes, who crashed near Kortewilde, northeast of Dixmuide, and died of severe head wounds in Steenbrugge hospital four days later. Dodds took his score to ten with three victories on 8 March 1918, and finished the war as a captain with the MC. Later attaining a high position in the Canadian transport bureaucracy, he died in Hamilton on 8 December 1980, aged 88. Tuffield survived the war with six victories.

2Lt Herbert Thomas and Sgt H F Watson of No 48 Sqn pose in Thomas' F 2B *Enid*. Note the pre-mission precaution *MT your pockets* painted on the Irish linen below the observer's pit. Thomas saw the wisdom of those words on 26 October 1918, when he and his observer, 2Lt F H V Coomer, were brought down and captured (*Herbert Thomas via Jon Guttman*)

Turned down for a flying position in New Zealand, Keith Park continued his career in the Royal Air Force, attaining a renown beyond his ace status in World War 2 as commander of No 11 Group, Fighter Command, during the Battle of Britain, and subsequently commanding fighter defences at Malta and serving in Burma. By the time he died back in his native New Zealand on 6 February 1975, the man who had entered aviation only because he had been invalided out of the army had retired as Air Chief Marshal Sir Keith Park.

'BIFF BOYS'

Its disastrous first combat notwithstanding, the Bristol Fighter soon earned the confidence of its crews. In time it came to be known by the popular nickname of 'Biff' for short, although it would later acquire another from the press – as W F J Harvey put it, 'that ugly nickname "Brisfit" in postwar years' – by which it came to be known by the general public, but seldom, if ever, by the men who had flown it.

By the time No 48 Sqn had sorted out how to make the best of its F 2As and newer F 2Bs, a second unit was acquiring Bristols. Formed at Netheravon, in Wiltshire, in February 1915, No 11 Sqn had been the RFC's first to be entirely equipped with fighters – and two-seaters at that, albeit Vickers FB 5 'Gunbus' pushers, followed by FE 2bs, occasionally complemented by single-seat DH 2s and Nieuport scouts. The squadron already boasted two VC recipients in its ranks – Lts Gilbert Stuart Martin Insall and Albert Ball – so there was plenty of tradition to live up to when the Bristols arrived in June 1917 and began adding significantly to the almost 300 victories credited to the unit by war's end.

Although no more of its personnel earned VCs, one of No 11 Sqn's pilots gained the distinction of being the highest scoring Bristol Fighter ace. Born in Lostowel, Ontario, on 21 August 1894, Andrew Edward McKeever entered the war as a member of the Canadian Expeditionary Force (CEF), gaining a reputation as a marksman in the trenches until December 1916, when he transferred to the RFC. He was posted to No 11 Sqn on 28 May 1917, just as the unit was exchanging its 'Fees' for Bristols. McKeever's first claim, with 2Lt E Oake as his observer, was over

F 2B A7131 displays the inward-sloping fuselage bars that marked No 11 Sqn's aeroplanes until 22 March 1918, as well as white wheel hubs and spinner which served as the flight colours. During earlier service in No 48 Sqn, A7131 was used by Lt Hugh William Elliott and 2Lt J W Ferguson to drive down an Albatros D V out of control over Slype on 21 July 1917, providing Elliott with the third of his five victories (*Philip Jarrett*)

two Albatros D Vs on 26 June, but his back-seater in the next – over three D Vs on 7 July – was 21-year-old 2Lt Leslie Archibald Powell, a former journalist with the *Western Daily Press* from Redland, Bristol, who would figure in the majority of his successes thereafter.

Flying with 2Lt E V deG Dodd, McKeever claimed a D V on 10 July and two more on the 13th, before reuniting with Powell to down three Albatros on 5 August. Yet another D V fell to his guns on 22 August, with 2Lt L F Ebbutt in the observer's pit, while on 11 September Powell shared in driving a D V down out of control near Cagnicourt with Capt Geoffrey Hooper from Sydney, New South Wales – the only victory Powell scored with someone other than McKeever as his pilot.

McKeever and Powell claimed two D Vs over Vitry on 23 September, and two days later McKeever and Dodd accounted for another. AM Hewitt backed McKeever up when he claimed three more D Vs on the 28th, as did Lt H G Kent when he destroyed a two-seater on 1 October. The next day, McKeever and Powell downed an Albatros D V in flames between Douai and Cambrai, and they claimed two more destroyed on the 16th. The following day, McKeever, whose score now stood at 20, was awarded the Bar to the MC he had received a month earlier (as had Powell). McKeever and Kent teamed up to down a D V on 20 October, he and Powell scored another Albatros 'hat trick' near Fresse on the 31st and on 11 November McKeever and Lt L V Pogson shared in the destruction of a DFW C V.

The exploits of Maj Andrew Edward McKeever of No 11 Sqn made him arguably the most famous Bristol Fighter pilot of them all, as well as the aircraft's highest-scoring exponent (*Stuart K Taylor*)

F 2B A7231 of No 11 Sqn was crewed by Lts Harry Scandrett and G Watson on 30 September 1917 when they drove down two Albatros D Vs out of control near Etaing for Scandrett's seventh, and last, victory. Born in 1892, Scandrett was living in Strawberry Hill, south London, when war broke out. He was serving in No 25 Sqn as an observer in FE 2b 7024 when he shared in the downing of an enemy aeroplane on 17 November 1916. Retrained as a pilot, Scandrett joined No 11 Sqn in the early summer of 1917. A7231 is shown here after being brought down southwest of Cambrai by Vzfw Karl Bey of *Jasta* 5 on 17 October 1917 (*Philip Jarrett*)

Vzfw Karl Bey poses before his Albatros D V at *Jasta* 5's aerodrome at Boistrancourt flanked by A7231's captured crew, pilot 2Lt E Scholtz (left) and observer 2Lt H C Wookey. Because the two had been carrying propaganda leaflets at the time, the Germans tried, convicted and sentenced Scholtz and Wookey to ten years' imprisonment for espionage (*Philip Jarrett*)

Besides providing invaluable data on the Bristol Fighter's capabilities, A7231 was refinished with German markings and pressed into service as *Jasta* 5's squadron hack (*Philip Jarrett*)

Concerned that black crosses would not be enough to deter trigger-happy fighter pilots from having a crack at its Bristol, *Jasta* 5 eventually added a highly visible entreaty to A7231's upper wings – '*Gute Leute nicht schiessen*!' ('Good people, don't shoot!') (*Philip Jarrett*)

Formidable though they were, Bristols were hardly invincible. F 2B A7130 of No 11 Sqn was brought down southwest of Sailly by Vzfw Friedrich Gille of *Jasta* 12 on 19 September 1917 for his sixth victory. The crew, 2Lt H T Taylor and Lt G W Mumford, was wounded and taken prisoner (*Norman Franks*)

McKeever and Powell flew in F 2B A7288 for their grand finale on 30 November. As McKeever's DSO citation described it;

'While on patrol by himself over enemy lines in very bad weather, he encountered two enemy two-seater machines and seven scouts. By skilful manoeuvring, he engaged one two-seater and destroyed it. As he turned to get back to the lines, five of the enemy dived on his tail, and his observer engaged and destroyed two of them. After an indecisive combat with two others, he attacked and destroyed one of the enemy which had overshot him. He continued the fight with the remainder until he was within 20 ft of the ground, when the enemy machines climbed and left him.'

This classic combat, which brought McKeever's total to 31 and Powell's to 19, became the model for the Bristol Fighter's reputation as a foe that German fighters would hesitate to attack in anything less than *Staffel* strength. It also left McKeever as the highest scoring 'Biff' pilot – a record to which some of his wartime successors would come tantalisingly close, but never quite exceed.

On 25 January 1918, McKeever and Powell – who added a Bar to his MC – were withdrawn to Home Establishment. Maj McKeever subsequently helped organise and commanded No 1 Sqn, Canadian Air Force, which was equipped with Sopwith Dolphins, but the war ended before the unit reached the front. In 1919, McKeever served as

Born on 27 June 1896, Leslie Archibald Powell came from Redland, Bristol, and had been a journalist with the *Western Daily Press* before the war. Joining No 11 Sqn on 16 July 1917, 2Lt Powell scored all but one of his 19 victories as observer to Capt Andy McKeever. The exception was an Albatros D V claimed with Australian Capt Geoffrey Herbert Hooper (11 victories) as his pilot on 11 September 1917 (*Norman Franks*)

Lts Andrew E McKeever and Harry Gowans Kent pose before F 2B A7121 of No 11 Sqn at Le Bellevue aerodrome in October 1917 (*H G Kent via Stuart K Taylor*)

manager at Mineola Field in New York, but on 3 September he was involved in a motoring accident, and after lingering for months, died of his injuries on Christmas Day 1919.

— DEATH OF AN ACE —

Although only a fraction of Bristol Fighter claims match enemy losses, No 11 Sqn could legitimately claim to have deprived the Germans of one of its aces on the very first day of their last major offensive in the West. *'Der Tag'*, launched on 21 March 1918, saw German *Jagdstaffeln* roaming the front to establish local air superiority in support of their advancing ground forces. Among the nine British aeroplanes and six balloons they claimed that day were two Camels of No 3 Sqn, credited at 1750 hrs to Ltn Ludwig Hanstein, commander of Royal Bavarian *Jasta* 35, and to *Staffel* mate Ltn Wolf *Freiherr* von Manteuffel-Szöge.

About ten minutes after scoring his 16th victory, however, Hanstein was killed around Vaulx-Noreuil, his Albatros D Va 5285/17 reportedly going down in flames. To further put a damper on *Jasta* 35b's day, as Ltn d R Karl Beyschlag limped back to his aerodrome at Emerchicourt, he became disoriented in the ground mist and crashed into a hangar, emerging shaken but miraculously unhurt from his wrecked machine.

The most likely description of Hanstein's fate came from the combat report of Lt H W Sellars of No 11 Sqn, flying F 2B C 4673 at that time;

'I next attacked a two-seater with a double tailplane, firing five bursts at 100 yards range as it dived eastwards over its line. We were then attacked from the rear by three Albatros Scouts. I did a sharp turn to the left, my observer firing two bursts at 75 yards range into the nearest enemy aircraft, which burst into flames and was seen to crash north of Morchies.'

The Hannover two-seater, which probably carried Vzfw Oscar Weiss and Lt d R Josef Szajsowski of *Flieger Abteilung (A)* 228 to their deaths, and Hanstein's Albatros were credited as the ace-making fifth and sixth victories for one of the few Bristol teams to stick together from start to unfortunate finish. Born in Westwork, Cheshire, in 1896, Herbert Whiteley Sellars received his RFC commission in June 1916 and joined No 25 Sqn on 2 August, but was injured in a crash on 16 September. Upon recovery, he rejoined the unit in July 1917, but on 19 October he transferred to No 11 Sqn.

Lt Herbert Whiteley Sellars scored all eight of his victories in concert with Lt Charles Crichton Robson in F 2B C4673, including downing 16-victory ace and commander of *Jasta* 35b Ltn Ludwig Hanstein. The team's luck ran out during a dogfight with *Jagdgeschwader* I on 15 May, when Sellars was killed and Robson taken prisoner (*Norman Franks*)

On 20 December, Edinburgh-born Lt Charles Crichton Robson, who had served in the 12th Regiment of the Royal Scots before joining the RFC, joined No 11 Sqn, and from then on became almost exclusively associated with Sellars and F 2B C4673. Their first victim was an LVG C VI over Doignes on 12 March, followed by Albatros D Vs on the 13th, 15th and 18th. Following their double victory on 21 March, the duo downed a Fokker Dr I on 2 April, and were flying F 2B C845 when they shared another triplane in a combat over Mametz at 1720 hrs (British time) on 15 May with Capt John Vincent Aspinall – a former infantryman of the Worcester Regiment for whom this was victory number six – and Lt P V de la Cour.

That last combat did not end well for the 'Biff boys', however, for their opponents were from *Jasta* 6 of *Jagdgeschwader* I – von Richthofen's 'Flying Circus' – and the equally deadly 'Green Tails' of *Jasta* 5, which occasionally flew with JG I at that time. One Bristol was shot down by Offz Stv Josef Mai of *Jasta* 5 over Contalmaison at 1815 hrs (German time) and the other was claimed by Ltn Hans Kirschstein of *Jasta* 6 over Orvillers five minutes later. Only Robson survived, to spend the rest of the war at Karlsrühe prison until his repatriation in December 1918 and his discharge from service on 28 February 1919. On 2 June Robson was gazetted for the MC – not for any combat per se, but for a long range reconnaissance mission completed in spite of poor weather conditions.

Another of No 11 Sqn's 'Canadians' was in fact 22-year-old American Eugene Seeley Coler from Newark, New Jersey. With Lt Cyril William Gladman, a 21-year-old former electrical engineer from Berkhamsted, Hertfordshire, as his observer, Coler's first success was a 'hat trick' of three Pfalz D IIIas sent down out of control on 9 May 1918, and the next time the duo scored would be over Péronne on 13 August – three Fokker D VIIs in flames and two more out of control in just a matter of three minutes!

The two met their match the next day, however, Coler being forced to land in Allied lines in D7912 with Gladman badly wounded, their demise possibly being caused by Ltn Otto Könnecke of *Jasta* 5. Coler was back in action by the 30th, flying E2215 for the remainder of his fighting career. That day, with 2Lt B E J D Tuke as his observer, he claimed a Fokker D VII and a Pfalz D XII destroyed northwest of Havrincourt. Lt D P Conyngham was in Coler's back seat on 6 September when they downed

Bristol F 2B C4844 of No 11 Squadron bore the legend *RICKADAMOGO* on its fuselage side (*Norman Franks*)

two Fokkers west of Cambrai, but Lt D J Corbett shared in his last two successful combats – two Fokkers on 15 September and a Pfalz D XII and a Fokker D VII the next day.

Coler had the unique distinction of never claiming fewer than two victories in a fight, but his luck ran out in that last one on 16 September, as No 11 Sqn took a beating from JG III. Two Bristols, claimed by Ltn Helmut Lange and Vzfw Otto Frühner of *Jasta* 26, fell in German lines, with 2Lts L Arnott and G L Bryars being killed and 1Lt Julian C Stanley (a pilot of the US Army Air Service, or USAS, assigned to No 11 Sqn) being wounded. He duly joined his observer, 2Lt E J Norris, in captivity.

In addition, the *Geschwaderkommandeur*, Oblt Bruno Loerzer, claimed one Bristol over Dourges, which was apparently Coler's, whose petrol tank was shot through and the aileron controls severed. Although wounded, Coler went into a power dive and pulled out at 1000 ft over Cambrai, where two of his pursuers overshot and he and Corbett claimed one each. Coler then limped his way back over the lines at 150 ft, finally sideslipping into the ground near Beugny. Although JG III recorded no pilots lost that day, Coler's last fight had been a testimony to his coolness under fire, and the durability of the Bristol F 2B.

After the war, Coler became a doctor in New York, but returned to his country's service during World War 2 as a bomber pilot with the 319th Bomb Group in North Africa. He later served with the Eighth Air Force in England. In 1951 Coler returned to England to serve as divisional air surgeon at Headquarters, 7th Air Division, where he remained until his premature death on 30 August 1953, having attained the rank of colonel in the US Air Force.

Another of No 11 Sqn's more notable aces, Geoffrey Herbert Hooper, was 24 when he enlisted in the Royal Engineers on 1 November 1915, transferring to the RFC in August 1916 and joining No 11 Sqn on 12 April 1917. He scored his first victory over an Albatros D III, with Capt F J Carr as his observer, on 26 June, and he had become a flight commander by the time he scored his third success with Leslie Powell. Awarded the MC on 18 September, Hooper was withdrawn for a rest and subsequently spent some time with No 38 Training Squadron, prior to returning to the front on 14 September 1918 as a flight commander with No 20 Sqn.

With 2Lt Harold Leslie Edwards as his observer, Hooper downed a Fokker D VII on 24 September, three on the 25th and three more on the 29th, adding one more for his 11th victory overall on 10 November. Hooper also had many day and night bombing missions to his credit when he was awarded the DFC in 1919. In 1923 he left the RAF to take a captaincy in the Royal Australian Air Force (RAAF).

Canadian Capt Carleton Main Clement had scored eight victories piloting FE 2bs with No 22 Sqn by the time it made the switch to Bristol F 2Bs. He then brought his tally up to 14, including four Albatros D Vs while flying A7172 on 12 August 1917. During an evening patrol on the 19th, however, Clement and Lt R B Carter were shot down and killed near Langemarck by anti-aircraft gunners from *Flakzug* 99. In addition to receiving the MC for his exploits in 'Fees', Clement was also awarded the *Croix de Guerre* (*Norman Franks*)

NEW UNIT

The third unit to acquire Bristols, No 22 Sqn had originally formed at Gosport, in Hampshire, in September 1915 and flown FE 2bs over France from April 1916 to July 1917, when it exchanged them for F 2Bs. While its predecessors had been expected to use their Bristols for armed reconnaissance missions as well as in a fighting role, No 22 Sqn put the emphasis on offensive patrolling and the escorting of bombers or reconnaissance aircraft. It claimed nearly 390 enemy aeroplanes and balloons by the end of the war, producing 27 pilots and seven observers with five or more victories.

Much personal detail of No 22 Sqn is known because one of its aces proved to have a literary bent. Born on 8 January 1898, William Frederick James Harvey had served in the Signal Company of the Royal Engineers before joining the RFC in December 1916. After training, he was posted to No 22 Sqn in December 1917, and with Sgt A Burton as his observer, claimed a Pfalz D III out of control on 16 March 1918. Two days later Harvey downed an Albatros D Va in flames with the aid of 2Lt Josiah Lewis Morgan.

Morgan, who hailed from Caerphilly, had served in the South Wales Borderers before transferring to the RFC on 10 October 1917 and joining No 22 Sqn on 13 January 1918. His usual pilot, Lt Hiram Frank Davison, was born in Leeds County, Ontario, on 12 January 1894, and had been a travelling salesman in Saskatchewan before the war. He then served as member of the Canadian Horse Artillery prior to joining the RFC. Davison and Morgan opened their joint account with an Albatros on 6 May, followed by three enemy fighters in a running fight between Lille and Douai two days later and a Pfalz on the 13th. After his fruitful sortie with Harvey, Morgan rejoined Davison to claim an Albatros on 25 March, a Pfalz the next day, two Fokker Dr Is on the 27th and a pair of two-seaters on the 29th.

It says something of No 22 Sqn's aggressive Bristol Fighter tactics that while Morgan shared the credit in 12 victories, only two enemy aeroplanes fell exclusively to his rear gun while he was teamed up with Davison, the latter personally accounting for the rest. Morgan returned to Home Establishment on 4 April, later receiving the MC for his work in ground strafing as well as air-to-air combat. After instructing at No 6 School of Aviation, he left the RAF on 11 April 1919. Meanwhile, only nine days after Morgan's departure, Hiram Davison was wounded on 13 April 1918 and saw no further combat. He eventually passed away in London, Ontario, in January 1974.

Seen warming up for take-off from Villeneuve-des-Vertues, F 2B B1152 shows the freshly painted-over remnants of its squadron bands, obliterated after 22 March 1918. Among this aeroplane's more notable crewmen were Lt Sydney Arthur Oades (who scored five of his 11 victories in it) and 2Lt Stanton W Bunting (five of seven) in February 1918, followed by Lt Hiram Frank Davison (for the first four of his 11 victories) and 2Lt J L Morgan on 8 March, and Sgt Ernest J Elton and 2Lt G S L Hayward, who downed two Albatros D Vs with it on 11 March (*Philip Jarrett*)

Capt W F J Harvey leads Bristols of No 22 Sqn's 'B' Flight on patrol from Serny aerodrome, in Artois, in June 1918. The pilots flying these aircraft are, from left to right, Harvey (26 victories) in 'G', Lt Herbert Howell Beddow (10 victories) in 'K', Lt G V Wheatley in 'J' and Lt Chester William McKinley Thompson (12 victories) (*Imperial War Museum via Colin A Owers*)

Meanwhile, 'Jim' Harvey had also 'made ace' during the hectic activity of the March 1918 *Kaiserschlacht*. With 2Lt J L Moore as his observer, he downed two Albatros D Vs south of Arras on 24 March, another Albatros the next day and burned a balloon northwest of Albert on the 30th.

By mid-May Harvey was a captain in command of 'B' Flight, and had a new observer in the form of Lt George Thomson, who had been born in England on 3 October 1896 but whose family had emigrated to Celista, British Columbia, in 1910. Thomson had previously served on the ground in the 30th Battalion CEF, 15th Battalion, 48th Highlanders of Canada and the 7/8th King's Own Scottish Borderers, being commissioned and twice wounded with the latter, before joining the RFC in October 1917 and being posted to No 22 Sqn on 19 March 1918. Thomson's first victories – a Pfalz on 8 May and two two-seaters on the 13th – were with Lt Stanley Harry Wallage, prior to Harvey becoming his regular pilot.

The duo resumed their scoring by burning two balloons around Bailleul on 20 May, downing a DFW out of control on the 22nd, a Pfalz on the 26th and two two-seaters destroyed on the 28th. Two triplanes on 10 July and three Fokker D VIIs on the 20th completed their collaboration, after which Harvey got Capt Dennis Edward Waight, who would be his observer for the remainder of his successes.

Born in London, Waight had earned an MC in the 12/13th Northumberland Fusiliers, before joining the RFC in March 1918. His first victory, a Pfalz on 10 July, was scored with Lt T W Martin, who had downed two Albatros D Vs the day before, and whose total would eventually reach six. During the British Amiens offensive of 8 August, Harvey and Waight shared in the destruction of two Pfalz D III as northeast of Vitry, followed by a Fokker D VII on the 11th, a Rumpler and a Pfalz on the 13th, a two-seater the next day, a Pfalz on the 16th, a two-seater on the 21st and a Halberstadt on the 22nd.

Waight would score twice more – a Fokker D VII on 31 August with five-victory South African ace Lt Ian Oliver Stead as his pilot, and a Pfalz D XII on 4 November that was the 12th victory for him, the 10th for his pilot, Capt Wallage, and the last for No 22 Sqn.

Besides his 26 credited victories, 18 of which he accounted for exclusively with his front gun, Jim

This rare in-flight shot of Harvey's F 2B 'G' (serial uncertain) was taken in June 1918. It shows the flight leader's pennants on the tailplane and the fuselage letter repeated beneath the wing in a black disc – a practice left over from No 22 Sqn's days flying FE 2bs (*Imperial War Museum via Colin A Owers*)

Harvey was the first pilot in the RAF to be awarded a Bar to his DFC. After postwar work as a flight instructor, he became a farmer, but returned to service in World War 2, for which he became a Member of the Most Excellent Order of the British Empire (MBE). Retiring to Kent thereafter, Harvey wrote articles for *Air Pictorial* magazine, as well as a history of No 22 Sqn, titled *Pi in the Sky*. He also served as President of the British branch of Cross & Cockade, a society of World War 1 aviation historians, from its inception in 1969 until his death on 21 July 1972.

LEADING ACE

The leading ace of No 22 Sqn, Samuel Frederick Henry Thompson had previously served with the Royal Army Service Corps prior to transferring to the RFC. He joined No 20 Sqn late in 1917, but did not get off to an encouraging start, crashing on 27 October. Subsequently transferred to No 22 Sqn, 'Siffy' Thompson and his observer, Lt Charles G Gass, drove an Albatros D V down out of control east of Merville, which was the first victory for both men. From then on, Thompson became increasingly aggressive, and more would be heard from his observer as well.

Born in Chelsea, London, in April 1898, Charles George Gass had initially served in the 2/24th London Regiment as a sergeant. He then got his commission in the 17th Battalion in October 1917 and was later transferred to the RFC, joining No 22 Sqn on 26 March 1918.

In late April No 22 Sqn got a new 'A' Flight leader of proven mettle by the name of Lt Alfred Clayborn Atkey. Born in Minebow, Saskatchewan on 16 August 1894, Atkey had worked at the *Toronto Evening Telegram* before the war, and after training in Nos 27 and 28 Reserve Sqns in early 1917, he joined No 18 Sqn on 8 September. Flying DH 4s with several bombardiers, Atkey acquired a reputation for handling the big aeroplane

Capt W F J Harvey checks the improvised overwing Lewis gun mounting on his F 2B E2466 at Agincourt on 1 July 1918. Capt Dennis Edward Waight, sitting in the observer's pit, was credited with 12 victories (*Jack Eder*)

Capt Alfred Clayburn Atkey (seated) was credited with a total of 38 victories – nine flying DH 4s and the rest in the Bristols of No 22 Sqn – while the 39 credited to Lt Charles George Gass (29 of which were scored whilst serving as Atkey's observer) made him the highest-scoring rear gunner in history (*Greg VanWyngarden*)

like a Sopwith Scout, claiming two enemy fighters on 4 February 1918, a Pfalz on 15 March, an Albatros the next day, a two-seater and a scout on 25 March, two Pfalz D IIIs on 12 April and another on the 21st. Soon after that, Atkey's squadron apparently decided that his talents would be better served in the cockpit of a Bristol Fighter. Upon arrival at No 22 Sqn, he chose Gass as his observer to form one of the most formidable two-seater teams in aviation history.

One of the most remarkable months in the first air war began on the evening of 7 May 1918, when Atkey and Gass, flying in company with Capt John E Gurdon and 2Lt Anthony John Hill Thornton, got into an engagement with an accumulation of enemy fighters northeast of Arras that came to be known in RAF annals as 'Two Against Twenty'. In the melée that ensued, Atkey and Gass claimed five of their antagonists in about as many minutes, while Gurdon and Thornton claimed another three, although German records list no corresponding fatalities.

John Everard Gurdon, who would become another leading Bristol exponent, was born in Balham, south London, on 24 May 1898, his family later moving to Surrey. In 1916 he left Tonbridge School to join the army and underwent an officer's education at Sandhurst. Commissioned in the Suffolk Regiment, Gurdon transferred to the RFC in May 1917, and in spite of an injurious crash during training, he got his wings and assignment to No 22 Sqn early in 1918.

At 1015 hrs on 8 May, Thompson, with Sgt L Kendrick as his observer, downed a two-seater and Gurdon temporarily teamed with Gass to down a DFW that afternoon. Atkey and Gass were reunited on 9 May for a reprise of their previous feat – albeit not in the same combat – when they claimed three enemy fighters over Lille at 0940 hrs and two Pfalz D IIIs north of Douai at 1840 hrs. Gurdon and Thornton also claimed a scout in the morning action, and Gurdon was in the evening fight too, with 2Lt A V Bollins as his gunner, downing three of the Pfalz, while Thompson and Kendrick accounted for another.

Atkey and Gass downed two Pfalz on 15 May, and the next day Thompson began a long team-up with 19-year-old Sgt Ronald Malcolm Fletcher by destroying three more Pfalz over Douai. Atkey and Gass

F 2B A7163 displays standard unit livery for No 22 Sqn prior to 22 March 1918 (*Greg VanWyngarden*)

F 2B C4810 'N' of No 22 Sqn, seen here in post-22 March 1918 markings – or rather, the lack of them – had been flown by Lt George W Bulmer and 2Lt Percy Stanley Williams to down two Pfalz D IIIs over Henin-Leitard at 1030 hrs on 16 March 1918. Bulmer would be credited with a total of ten victories by war's end, and Williams with seven (*Norman Franks*)

despatched three two-seaters on 19 May and a trio of Halberstadt two-seaters the following day. Thompson and Fletcher downed two Pfalz on the 21st and single Albatros D Vas on the 22nd and 25th.

Atkey and Gass resumed their rampage with three Pfalz on 27 May, two on the 30th, two on the 31st and two two-seaters on 2 June. Atkey was posted home after that, and was awarded the MC and Bar. He died on 10 February 1971, little known in spite of being the highest-scoring two-seater pilot of the war with 38 victories, 29 of which were in Bristols.

Gass' score stood at 31 when Atkey left, but he was not quite finished. Meanwhile, Thompson and Fletcher continued their scoring, with a two-seater and an Albatros D V on 1 June and two Pfalz on the 2nd, the latter date also seeing Lt Ernest C Bromley down a pair of two-seaters, bringing his score to ten and that of his usual observer, 20-year-old Londoner 2Lt John Howard Umney, to 12.

Bromley had Gass in his observer's pit at 1030 hours on 5 June when he destroyed a Halberstadt south of Laventie, Gass then fending off an attacking Albatros D Va, which he sent down out of control. Two more Albatros fell to Thompson and Fletcher in that action, while a third was claimed by Gurdon and Sgt John Herbert Hall, the latter being a mechanic who had volunteered for observer duties with No 22 Sqn. In a later patrol that day, Gurdon and Hall destroyed a Pfalz in flames over Fromilly at 1915 hrs.

Thompson and Fletcher scored another double on 23 June, as did Gurdon, who had 18-year-old 2Lt James McDonald from Renfrew, in Scotland, as his observer. Gurdon then took on a new observer in the person of 19-year-old 2Lt James John Scaramanga from Redhill, in Surrey, who had failed to qualify as a pilot, but had scored two victories with No 20 Sqn prior to being wounded on 11 April 1918 and transferring to No 22 Sqn upon his recovery. The pair downed a Pfalz on 1 July, a Fokker D VII on the 4th and a DFW on the 9th.

Gurdon and Scaramanga had a run-in with Pfalz D IIIas between Armentières and Lille at 0930 hrs on 10 July, when they claimed two opponents before being badly shot up, Gurdon being hit in the arm and Scaramanga losing consciousness from his severe wound. With one Pfalz on his tail and closing for the kill, Gurdon used his one good arm to whip his Bristol around and shoot his assailant down out of control. Gurdon managed to make it home, but Scaramanga died of his wound shortly after landing and was buried at Aire. No German claims over Bristols (not even a probable) have come to light, but Ltn August Hartmann of *Jasta* 30 was slightly wounded and Ltn Wilhelm Oberstadt of *Jasta* 56 severely wounded that day, suggesting that either or both units could have been involved in the fight.

Thompson reunited with Gass to down a Fokker Dr I on 26 July. Gurdon flew with Gass to down an Albatros over Douai on 8 August, followed by a Pfalz in flames, shared with Capts Harvey and D E Waight. Gurdon and Gass added two Fokker D VIIs to their tallies on the 10th and a third on the 13th. Gass was withdrawn for pilot training soon afterward, but the war ended before he could return to the front. He left the service on 11 April and lived his later years in south London, the war's highest-scoring observer with 39 enemy aeroplanes to his credit.

Gurdon's victory on 13 August was his 28th, but soon after that the concussion of a close-bursting anti-aircraft shell, combined with his earlier wound, rendered him unfit for further flying. Awarded the DFC, he returned to England in September and resigned his commission on 21 December 1918.

Capt John Everard Gurdon scored 28 victories with No 22 Sqn between 2 April and 13 August 1918, earning the DFC and Bar before a concussion from a close anti-aircraft burst, added to an arm wound suffered on 10 June, rendered him unfit for further combat (*Norman Franks*)

Gurdon's sister Mary married his squadronmate Jim Harvey in August 1920. Gurdon himself married in 1921, and two of his three sons saw action with the RAF during World War 2 – one, Sgt John Robert Gurdon, was killed aboard a Wellington of No 166 Sqn on 11 April 1943, and the other, Philip F Gurdon, flew Spitfires in Burma.

John Gurdon, in spite of being blinded in one eye in a road accident in 1935 and suffering a hip injury in an air crash, served as an instructor and lecturer during World War 2. He managed to wangle a combat mission in the front turret of a Wellington, but his aeroplane was struck in a tyre by enemy flak, ground looped upon landing and ended up on its nose. The crash aggravated Gurdon's hip injury to the point that he was once again invalided out of the RAF. John Gurdon died in Alassio, Italy, on 14 April 1973.

While Gurdon was finishing up his scoring, Thompson and Fletcher were accounting for another three enemy fighters on 13 August 1918, to which they added two Fokker D VIIs on the 27th, one on 2 September, two more on the 5th and another on the 24th. 'Siffy' Thompson's final victory (a Halberstadt north of Noyelles) was achieved with 2Lt Clifford John Tolman in the back seat at 0720 hrs on 27 September, but during an afternoon sortie the pair was killed east of Cambrai by either Oblt Otto Schmidt of *Jasta* 5 or Vzfw Oskar Hennrich of *Jasta* 46.

Cliff Tolman, from Whippingham, on the Isle of Wight, was 21, and had scored seven victories as observer to Lt Frederick Cecil Stanton prior to that last sortie. At the time of his death at age 28, Thompson's score totalled 30 – a record for a Bristol pilot second only to Andy McKeever's.

There was a second ace named Thompson in No 22 Sqn – Chester William McKinley Thompson, who, after being commissioned on 27 September 1917, joined the unit in the spring on 1918 and opened his account on 28 May, when he and his observer, Sgt Hubert Cecil Hunt, sent an enemy two-seater down out of control. Both men would not score again until August, with different teammates. Hunt's pilot was

Airmen of No 22 Sqn empty their pockets before departing on patrol. These men are, from left to right, A P Stayle, Ian Oliver Stead (5 victories), H J Weaver, Herbert H Beddow (10), W F J Harvey (26), John E Gurdon (28), George W M Thomson (14) and George W Bulmer (10) (*Norman Franks*)

Lt Thomas Henry Newsome when they destroyed two Fokker D VIIs on 8 August. Thompson had 2Lt J Amos in the back seat when he claimed a D VII on 11 August and a Pfalz two days later. Lt Cyril Edward Hurst then teamed with Hunt to score all five of his victories – a two-seater on 16 August, a Fokker Dr I and two Pfalz scouts on the 25th and a Fokker D VII on the 31st.

Thompson, now with former Royal Irish Rifles member 2Lt G McCormack in the back, destroyed a Pfalz on 3 September, a Fokker D VII on the 5th, two more on the 17th and one on the 24th. Thompson and Lt W R James downed a D VII on the 25th, but Lt William Upton Tyrrell, another veteran of the Royal Irish Rifles, was Thompson's observer when he claimed two Fokkers on the 26th. On the 27th, Thompson and James shared in the destruction of a D VII with Lts L C Rowney and Tyrrell for Thompson's 12th and Tyrrell's sixth victories.

Sgt Ernest John Elton shows off the DCM and MM that he was awarded for his outstanding performance as mechanic and Bristol Fighter pilot. Elton passed away in Taplow, Buckinghamshire, on 8 March 1958 (*Norman Franks*)

During a fight between No 22 Sqn and *Jasta* Boelcke around midday on the 29th, however, Thompson and James were shot down in F 2B E2517 east of Cambrai, probably victims of Uffz

Karl Fervers, and taken prisoner. In addition, 1Lt Earl Adams (a USAS pilot attached to the squadron) and Sgt G H Bissell were killed, probably by Vzfw Paul Keusen.

No roster of No 22 Sqn's most distinguished pilots can be complete without Ernest John Elton. Born in Wimborne, Dorset, on Christmas Day 1893, he had entered the RFC as an air mechanic in 1915 and helped design and build the machine gun mount, firing forward at an angle to clear the propeller blades, on the Bristol Scout in which Capt Lanoe G Hawker scored his first three victories and earned the VC in July of

A line-up of pilots and observers from No 22 Squadron on 1 April 1918. The aces in this group are, third from left, Capt Stanley Harry Wallage (10 victories), fifth from left 2Lt George Searle Lomax Hayward (24), seventh from left 2Lt Roland Critchley (7), who was killed by a Fokker Dr I of *Jasta* 11 on 2 April 1918, eighth from left Capt W F J Harvey (26), ninth from left Lt Josiah Lewis Morgan (12), tenth from left Lt Hugh Fitzgerald Moore (6), eleventh from left Lt Hiram Frank Davison (11), twelfth from left Capt John E Gurdon (28) and seventeenth from left Capt David McKay McGoun (9) (*Norman Franks*)

Sgt E J Elton works the added Lewis gun mount above his pilot's cockpit while his observer, 2Lt Roland Critchley, mans a double Lewis mounting on the Scarff ring in F 2B B1162 'F' of No 22 Sqn in late March 1918. Elton scored 16 victories and had obtained a commission by war's end, while Critchley was credited with seven enemy aeroplanes (*Norman Franks*)

Lt William Lewis Wells scored six victories with No 22 Sqn between 25 January and 16 March 1918 – accounting for three Pfalz D IIIs on the last date – and was then posted to No 48 Sqn as a captain and flight commander. There, he downed a Pfalz D III on 21 March and two LVGs and a Pfalz two days later, but he was hit on the 28th and died of his wounds on 6 May. Wells was awarded the MC a week later, to which a Bar was subsequently announced (*Norman Franks*)

that same year. Eventually gaining acceptance for pilot training himself, Sgt Elton was posted to No 22 Sqn early in 1918. With Sgt John Charles Hagen as his observer, Elton began his own scoring by destroying two Albatros D Vs east of Lens on 26 February, only to be shot down without injury in Allied lines.

With 2Lt George Searle Lomax Hayward as his observer, Elton claimed two more Albatros on 6 March, another on the 8th with observer Sgt S Belding, and with Hayward in the back again, two Albatros on 11 March, and an Albatros and a Pfalz on the 13th. With Lt Roland Critchley from Fairhaven, Blackpool, as his final observer, Elton destroyed two Albatros D Vs on the 16th, one on the 18th, a Pfalz on the 26th and three two-seaters on the 29th.

Although it took a while for him to receive what was a thoroughly deserved commission, Sgt Elton was awarded the Distinguished Conduct Medal (DCM) and Military Medal (MM) from Britain and the *Medaglia di Bronzo al Valore Militare* from Italy for his feat of downing 16 enemy aeroplanes, ten of them with his front gun, in just 32 days.

Two of Elton's observers were also classed as aces, but Roland Critchley did not survive long afterward. On 2 April his flight had a run-in with *Jasta* 11, two Bristols falling victim to Ltns Hans Joachim Wolff and Hans Weiss. The 'Biff' crewmen, 2Lts E D James, R F Newton, F Williams and Critchley, were all killed.

George Hayward, who had previously served as a lance corporal in the Royal West Kent Regiment before getting his commission on 28 September 1916 and subsequently transferring into the RFC, had already scored two victories with 2Lt W G Pudney as his pilot. After the six he shared with Elton, he flew with Lt William Lewis Wells to claim two Pfalz and one Albatros on 16 March. Wells, whose score then stood at six, duly transferred to No 48 Sqn and scored four more victories in the F 2B prior to being badly shot up on 28 March and eventually dying of his wounds on 6 May.

Meanwhile, Hayward teamed up with 2Lt Frank Gerald Craven Weare, a former member of the East Kent Regiment ('The Buffs') to increase his total to 24 by 22 April, when they sent two Albatros D Vs down out of control east of Merville.

It should be noted again, however, that Hayward's rear Lewis only figured in four of the team's 13 victories – 'Weary' Weare's front gun had accounted for 11 of the total of 15 enemy aeroplanes with which he was credited by then. Both Weare and Hayward were awarded MCs for their success in the F 2B, and Weare went on to attain the rank of lieutenant colonel by the time he retired from the army. In civilian life he was a justice of the peace and a member of the Tunbridge Wells Council, prior to his death on 6 July 1971.

Capt Frank Gerald Craven Weare used his front gun to score 11 of his 15 victories with No 22 Sqn between 13 March and 22 April 1918, the other four falling to his usual observer, 2Lt G S L Hayward, whose own accredited total came to 24. In postwar years 'Weary' Weare became a justice of the peace and a member of the Tunbridge Wells Council prior to his death on 6 July 1971 (*Norman Franks*)

COLOUR PLATES

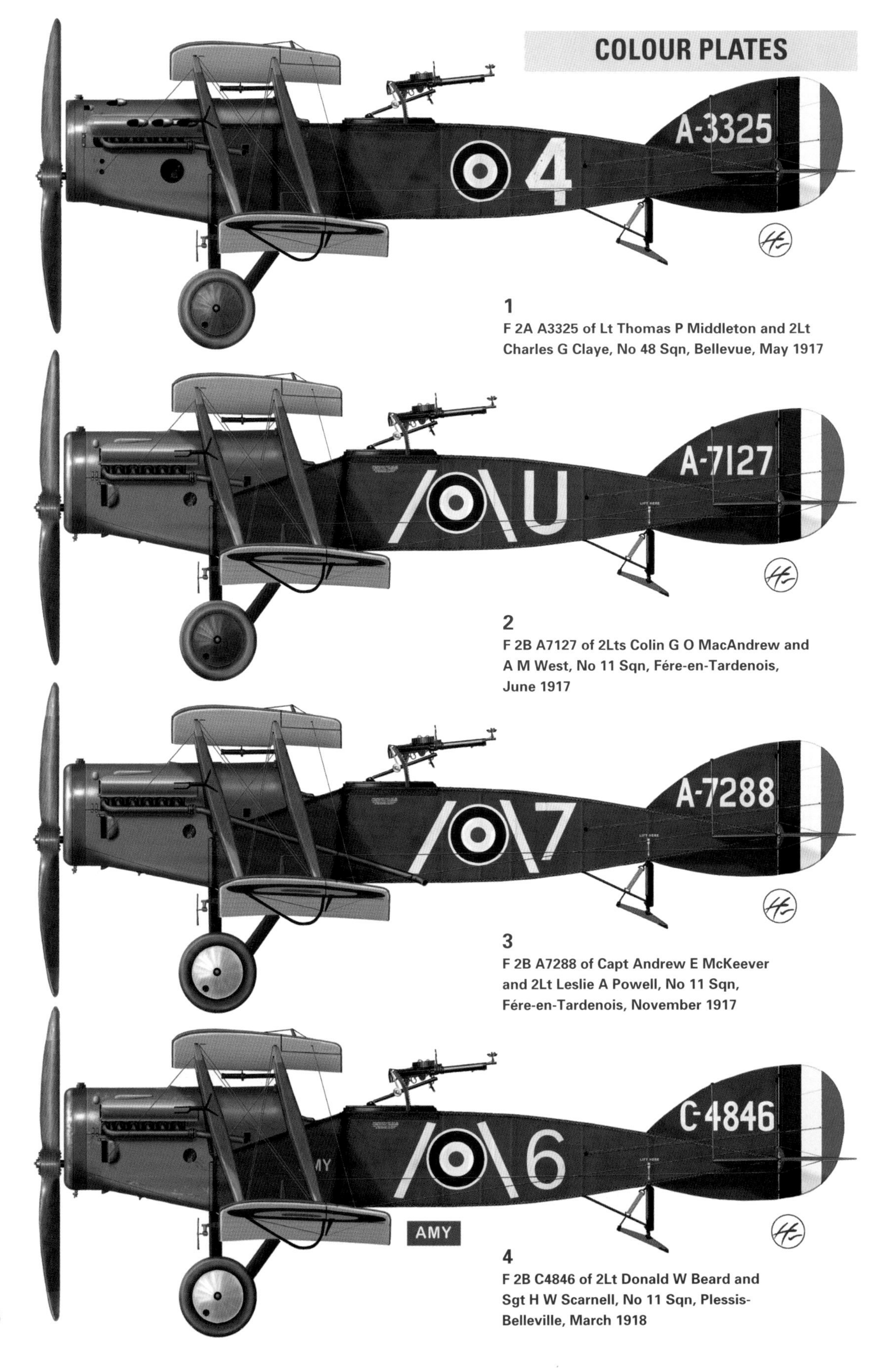

1
F 2A A3325 of Lt Thomas P Middleton and 2Lt Charles G Claye, No 48 Sqn, Bellevue, May 1917

2
F 2B A7127 of 2Lts Colin G O MacAndrew and A M West, No 11 Sqn, Fére-en-Tardenois, June 1917

3
F 2B A7288 of Capt Andrew E McKeever and 2Lt Leslie A Powell, No 11 Sqn, Fére-en-Tardenois, November 1917

4
F 2B C4846 of 2Lt Donald W Beard and Sgt H W Scarnell, No 11 Sqn, Plessis-Belleville, March 1918

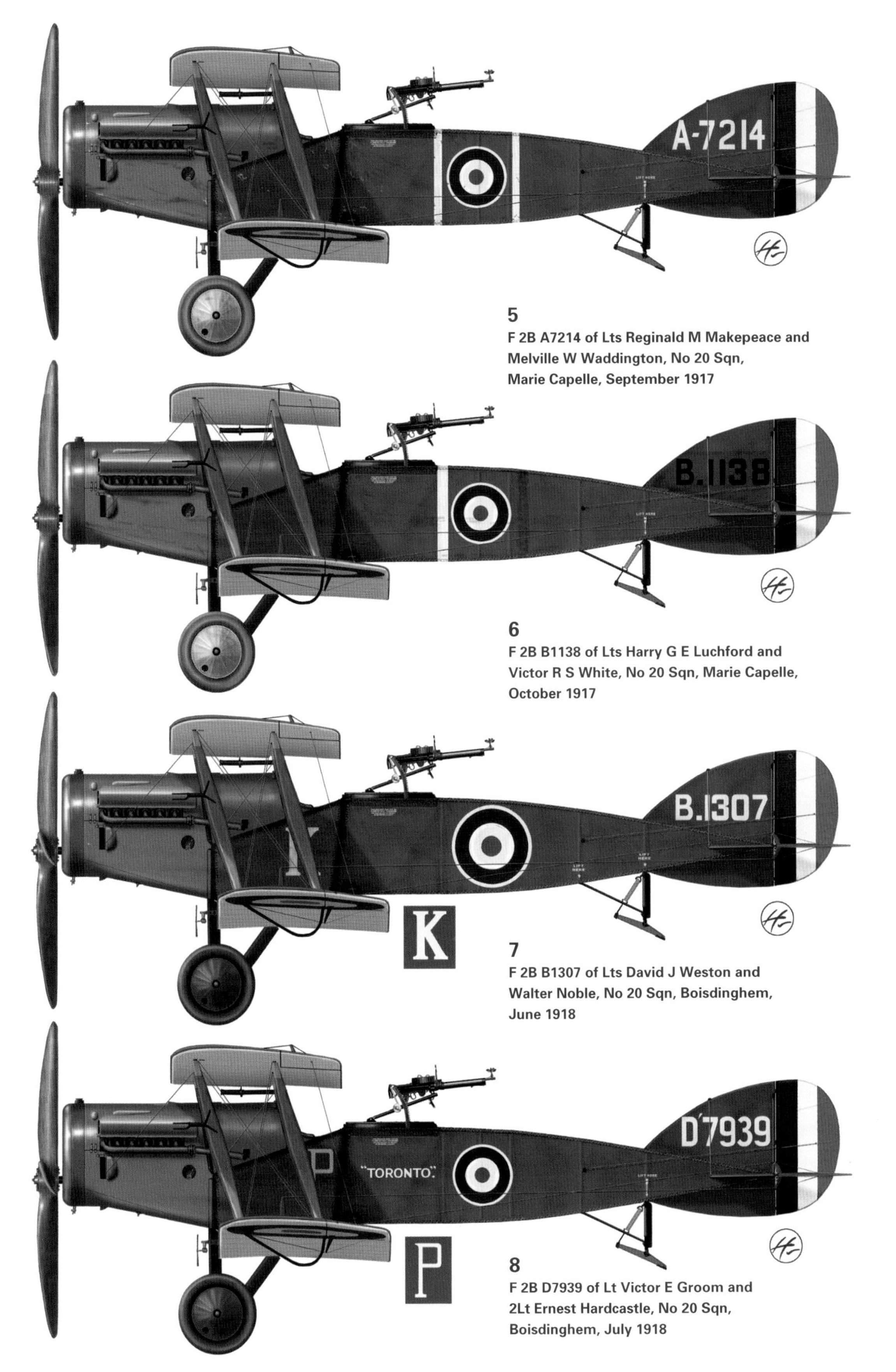

5
F 2B A7214 of Lts Reginald M Makepeace and Melville W Waddington, No 20 Sqn, Marie Capelle, September 1917

6
F 2B B1138 of Lts Harry G E Luchford and Victor R S White, No 20 Sqn, Marie Capelle, October 1917

7
F 2B B1307 of Lts David J Weston and Walter Noble, No 20 Sqn, Boisdinghem, June 1918

8
F 2B D7939 of Lt Victor E Groom and 2Lt Ernest Hardcastle, No 20 Sqn, Boisdinghem, July 1918

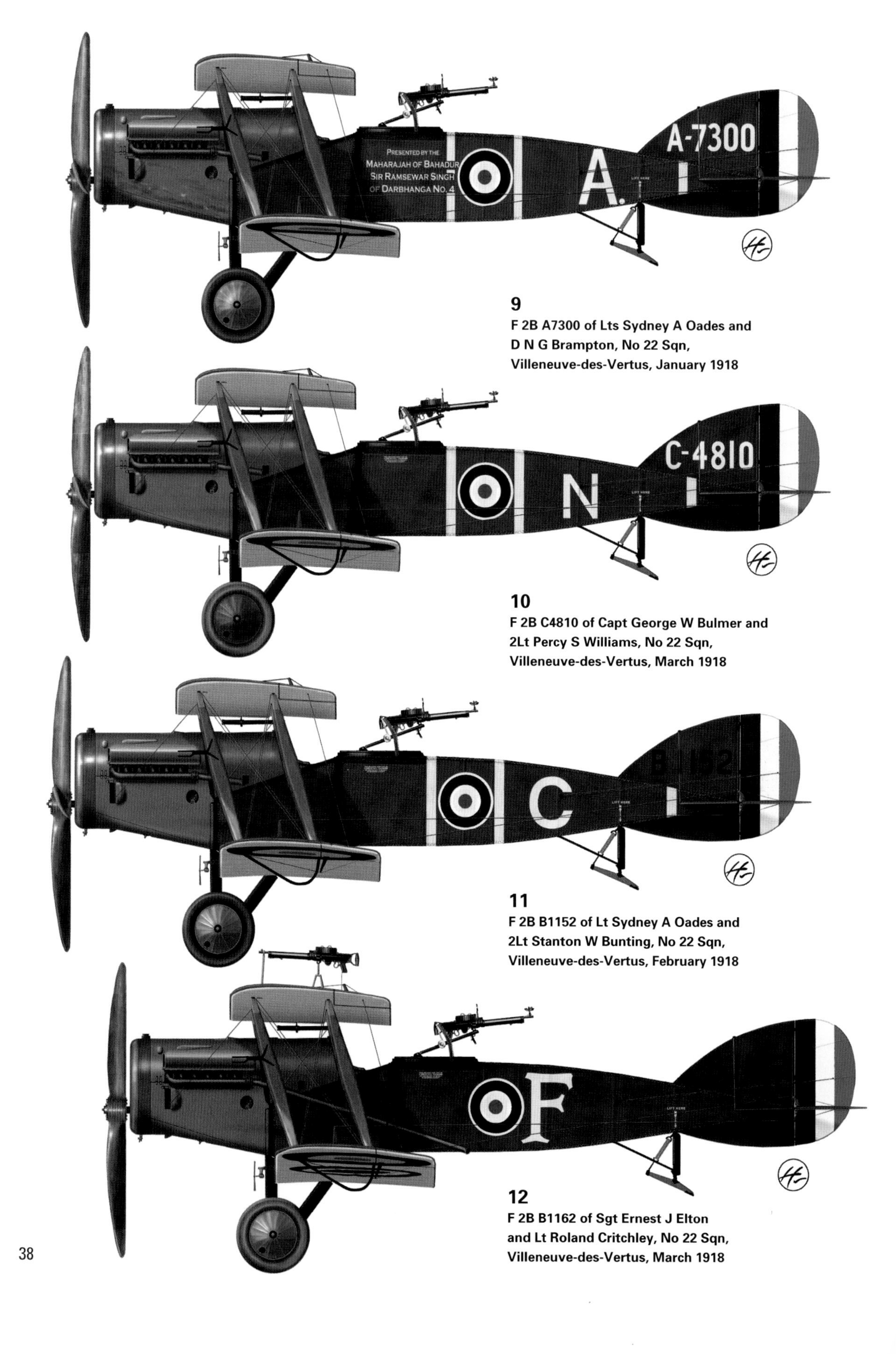

9
F 2B A7300 of Lts Sydney A Oades and D N G Brampton, No 22 Sqn, Villeneuve-des-Vertus, January 1918

10
F 2B C4810 of Capt George W Bulmer and 2Lt Percy S Williams, No 22 Sqn, Villeneuve-des-Vertus, March 1918

11
F 2B B1152 of Lt Sydney A Oades and 2Lt Stanton W Bunting, No 22 Sqn, Villeneuve-des-Vertus, February 1918

12
F 2B B1162 of Sgt Ernest J Elton and Lt Roland Critchley, No 22 Sqn, Villeneuve-des-Vertus, March 1918

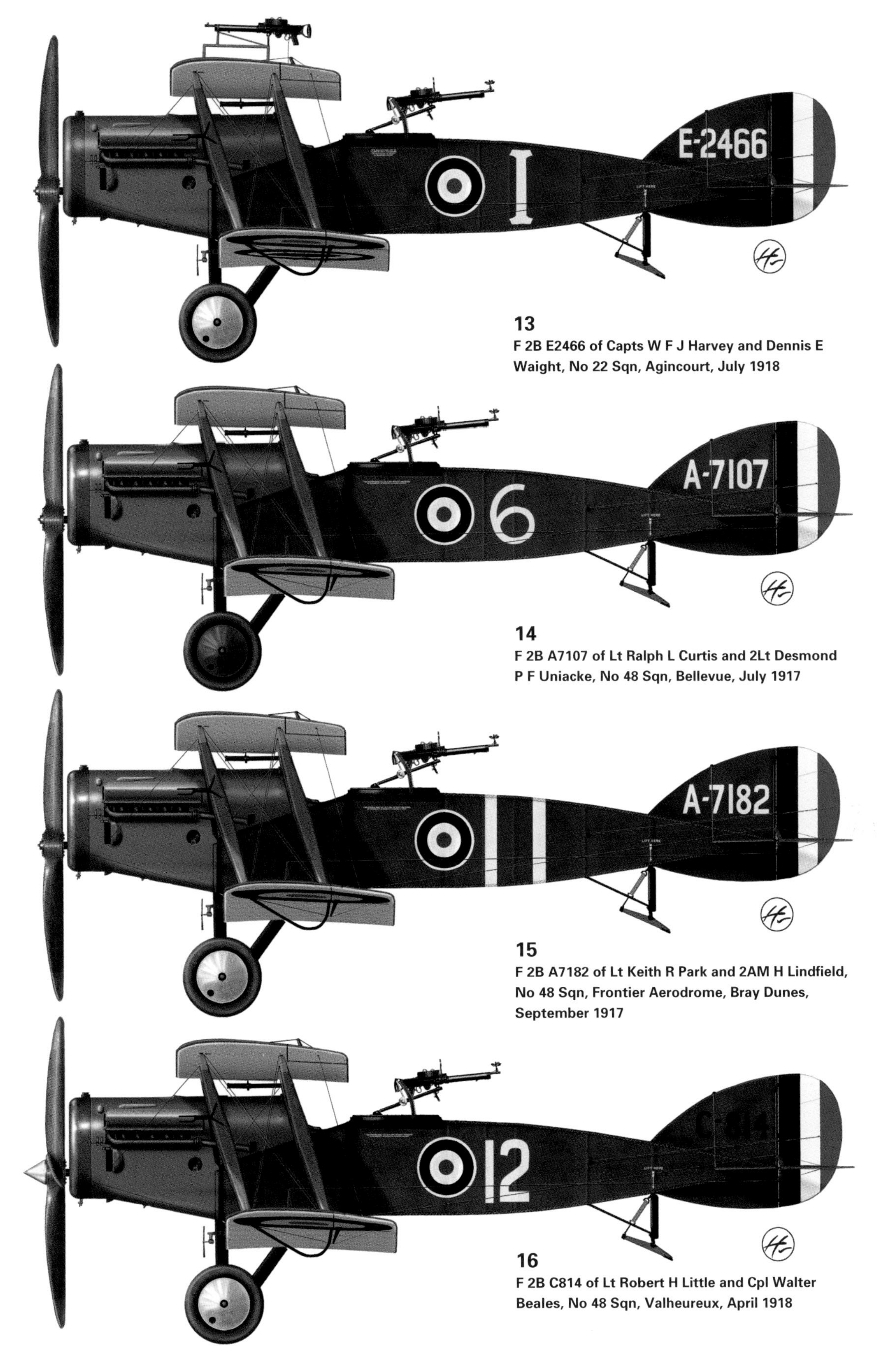

13
F 2B E2466 of Capts W F J Harvey and Dennis E Waight, No 22 Sqn, Agincourt, July 1918

14
F 2B A7107 of Lt Ralph L Curtis and 2Lt Desmond P F Uniacke, No 48 Sqn, Bellevue, July 1917

15
F 2B A7182 of Lt Keith R Park and 2AM H Lindfield, No 48 Sqn, Frontier Aerodrome, Bray Dunes, September 1917

16
F 2B C814 of Lt Robert H Little and Cpl Walter Beales, No 48 Sqn, Valheureux, April 1918

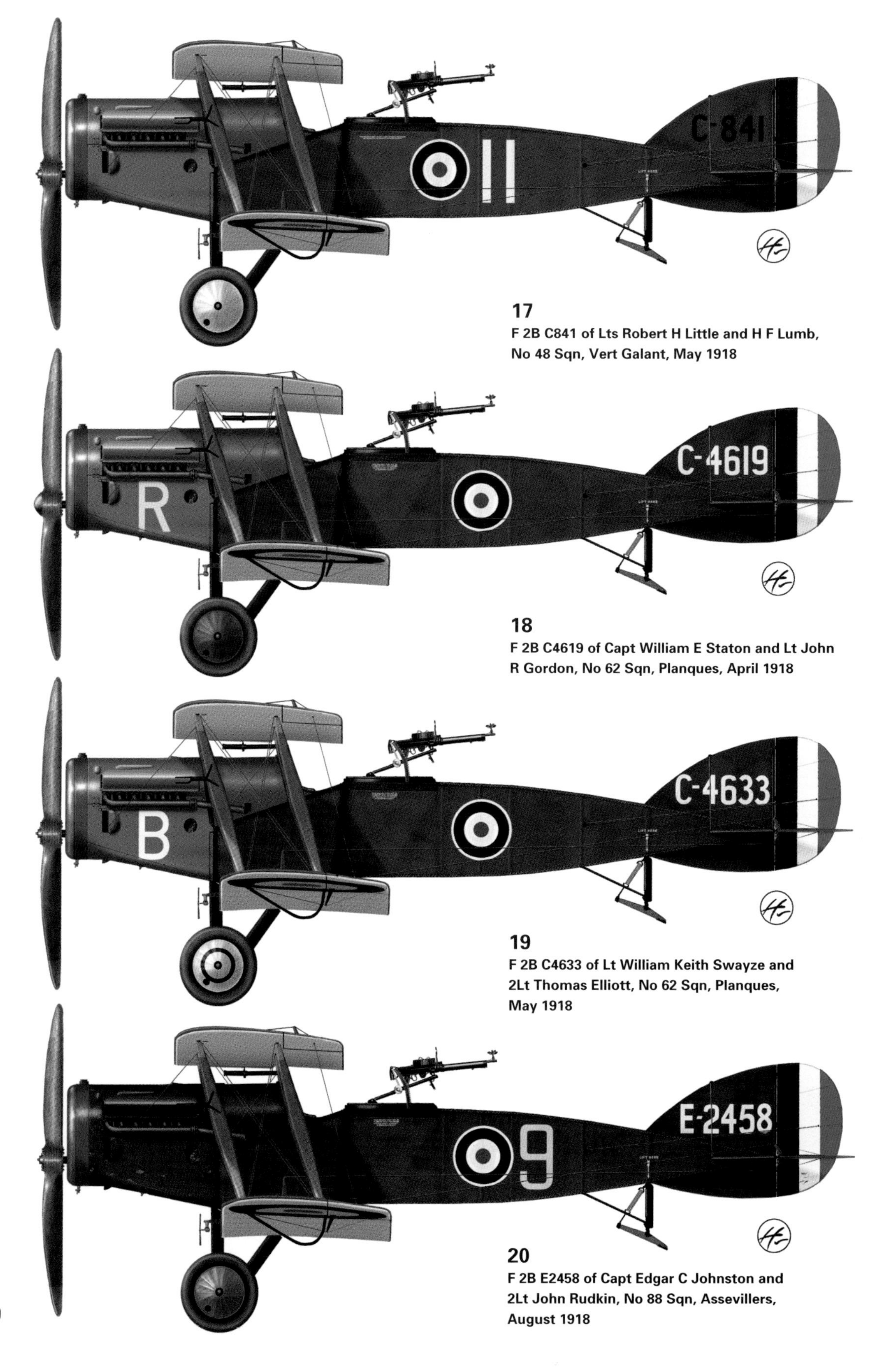

17

F 2B C841 of Lts Robert H Little and H F Lumb, No 48 Sqn, Vert Galant, May 1918

18

F 2B C4619 of Capt William E Staton and Lt John R Gordon, No 62 Sqn, Planques, April 1918

19

F 2B C4633 of Lt William Keith Swayze and 2Lt Thomas Elliott, No 62 Sqn, Planques, May 1918

20

F 2B E2458 of Capt Edgar C Johnston and 2Lt John Rudkin, No 88 Sqn, Assevillers, August 1918

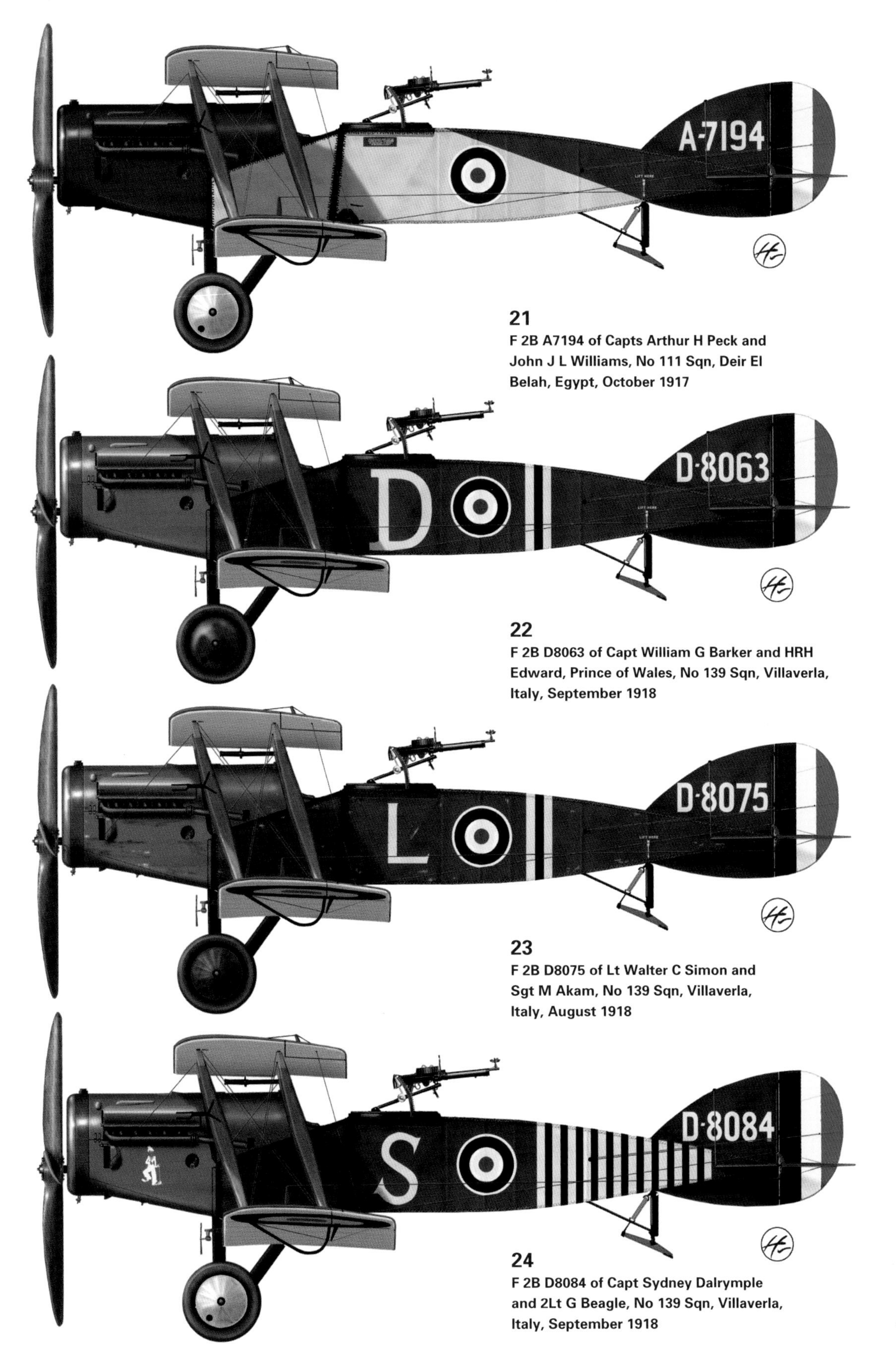

21
F 2B A7194 of Capts Arthur H Peck and John J L Williams, No 111 Sqn, Deir El Belah, Egypt, October 1917

22
F 2B D8063 of Capt William G Barker and HRH Edward, Prince of Wales, No 139 Sqn, Villaverla, Italy, September 1918

23
F 2B D8075 of Lt Walter C Simon and Sgt M Akam, No 139 Sqn, Villaverla, Italy, August 1918

24
F 2B D8084 of Capt Sydney Dalrymple and 2Lt G Beagle, No 139 Sqn, Villaverla, Italy, September 1918

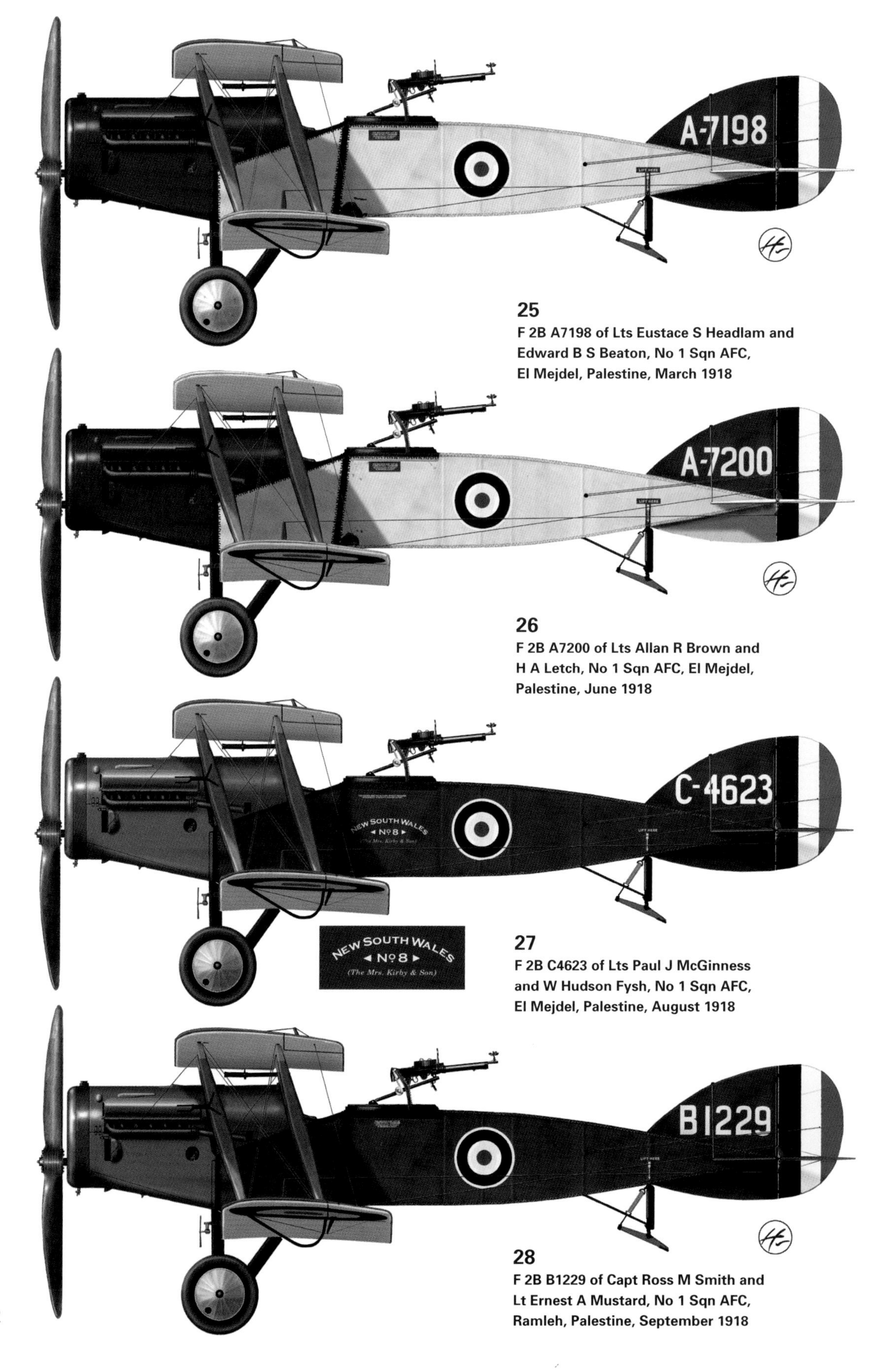

25
F 2B A7198 of Lts Eustace S Headlam and Edward B S Beaton, No 1 Sqn AFC, El Mejdel, Palestine, March 1918

26
F 2B A7200 of Lts Allan R Brown and H A Letch, No 1 Sqn AFC, El Mejdel, Palestine, June 1918

27
F 2B C4623 of Lts Paul J McGinness and W Hudson Fysh, No 1 Sqn AFC, El Mejdel, Palestine, August 1918

28
F 2B B1229 of Capt Ross M Smith and Lt Ernest A Mustard, No 1 Sqn AFC, Ramleh, Palestine, September 1918

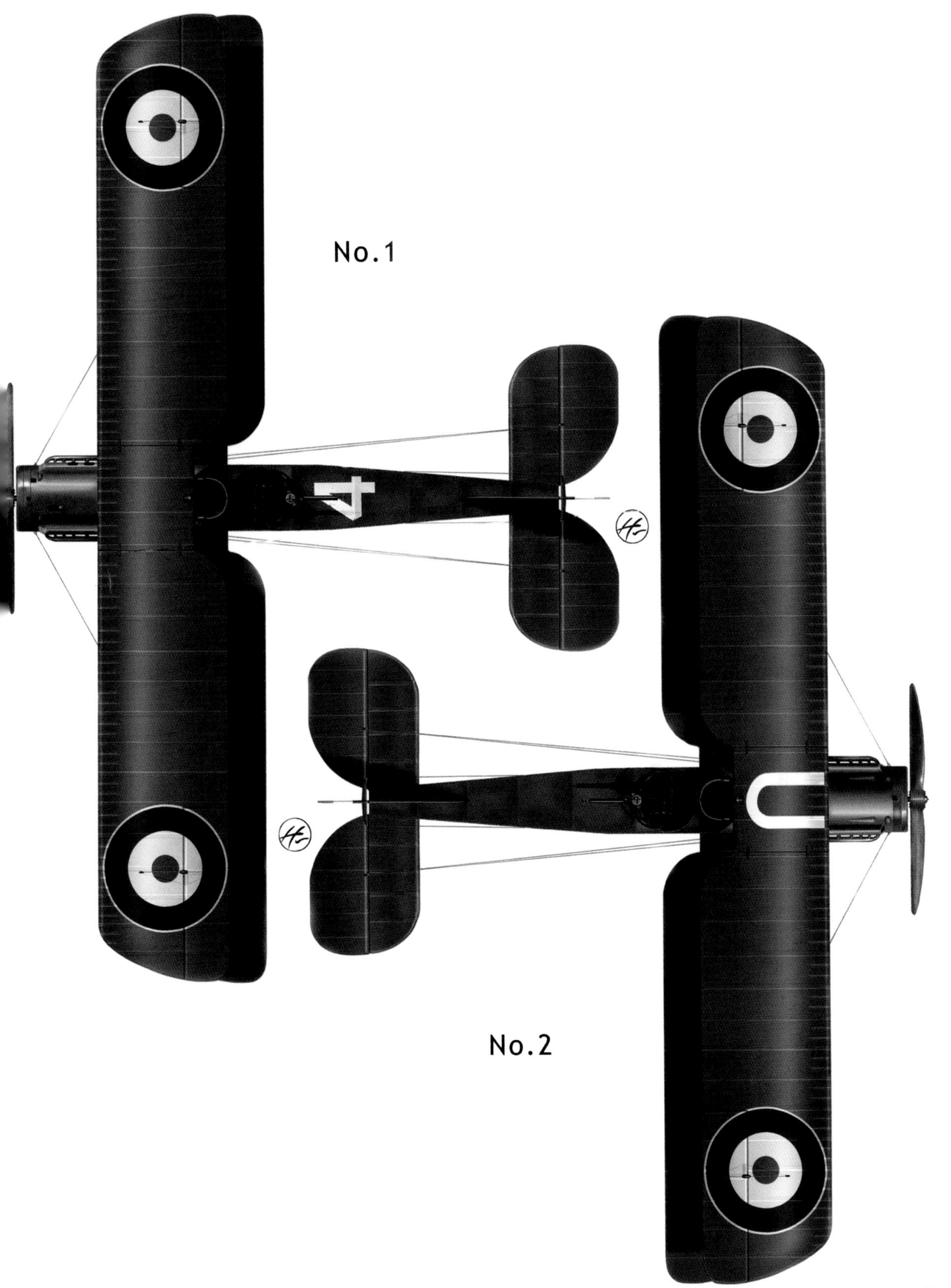
No.1
No.2

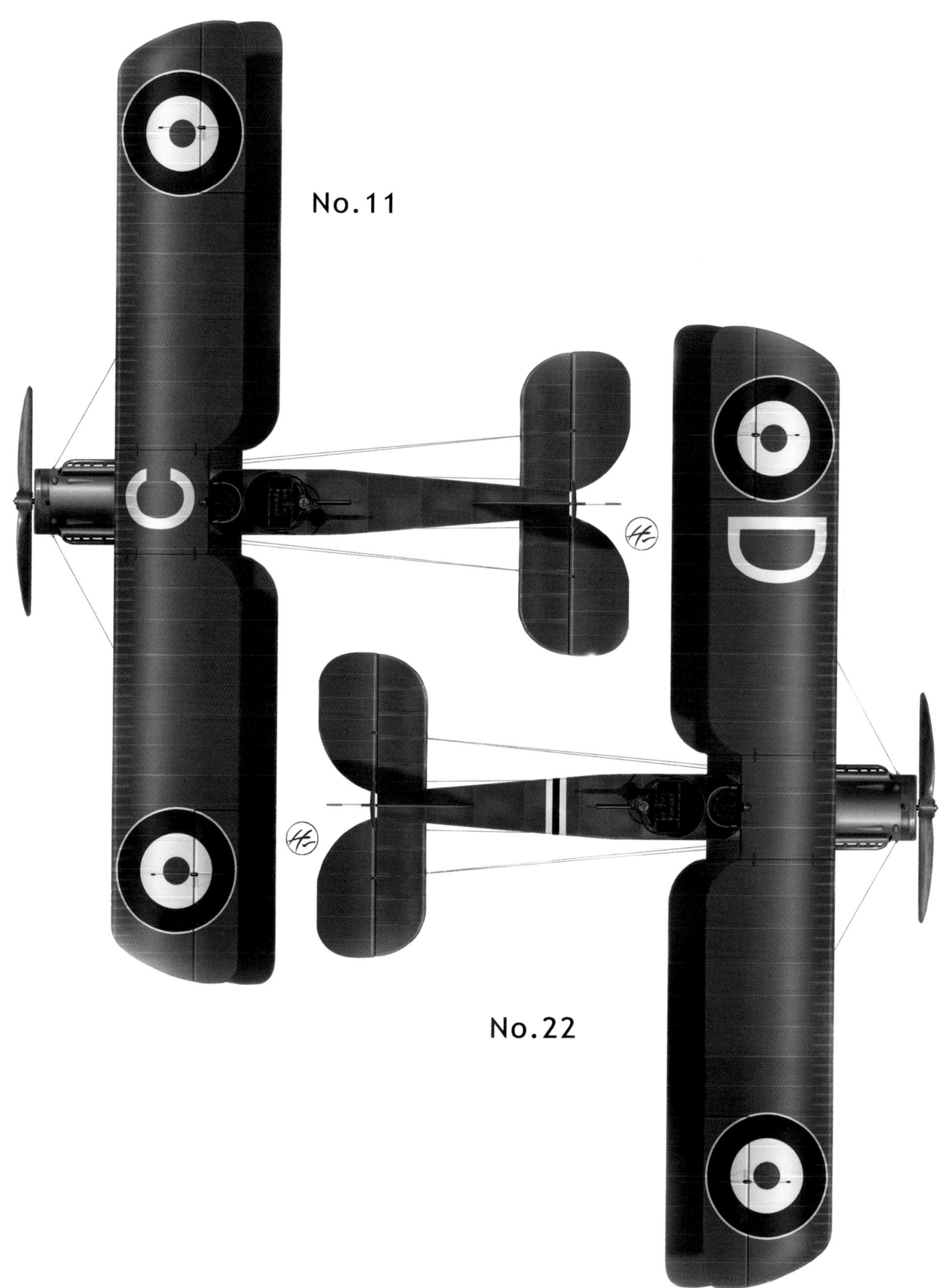
No.11
C
D
No.22

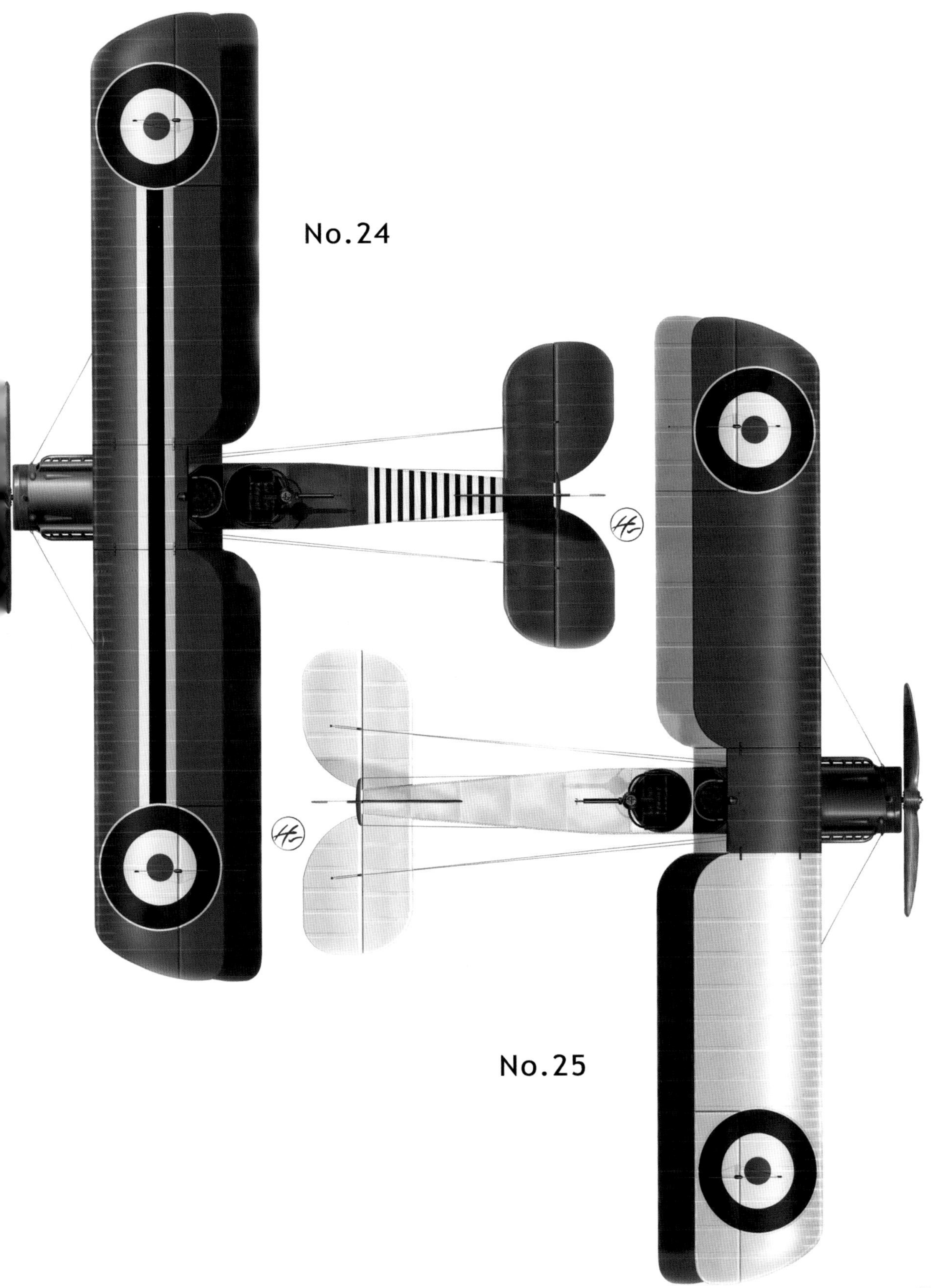
No.24
No.25

PLAIN LETHAL

If one accepts its official score, No 20 Sqn stands as the most successful fighter unit of World War 1, with 138 victories credited to its pilots and 481 to its observers, for a grand total of 619. That said, it must also be borne in mind that the squadron's victories, like those of previously mentioned units, were a reflection not only of the skill and courage of the men who claimed them, but of the relatively lax policies by which the British confirmed and counted them.

In addition to a 'crashed' or 'destroyed' machine, a 'decisive combat' for a British aircrew could take the form of an enemy aeroplane driven down 'out of control' or 'OOC', and in all cases the witnesses' testimony required to confirm such a kill, almost invariably made behind enemy lines, was far less strict than the requirements of the French or the Germans (the latter of whose confirmation tasks were conversely eased by most of the fighting taking place over their territory).

A stunning discrepancy occurs whenever one compares British claims with recorded German losses on a given day. Even allowing for the fact that German loss records only listed dead, wounded or missing crewmen rather than destroyed or damaged aircraft with any consistency, comparing the overall claims made by British squadrons and their aircrews with known German production figures leaves an inescapable impression that if the British claims were true, there would have been no enemy aeroplanes left over the Western Front, let alone a viable and still dangerous opposing force by war's end.

Accepting No 20 Sqn's score as being at least made in good faith does provide enthusiasts of the period's aviation with the irony of the war's top-scoring squadron being among the drabbest-looking, even by RFC or RAF standards. In contrast to the kaleidoscope of colours that identified German scouts or the whimsical insignias and large numerals that graced the sides of French and American aircraft, No 20 Sqn seemed only grudgingly inclined to give its aeroplanes more than the minimum required beyond the cockades and serial number.

Initially No 20 Sqn identified its 'Biffs' with a white band fore and aft of the fuselage cockade, reducing it to just one forward of the national marking by December 1917. The day after the Germans launched their final all-out bid for victory in the West on 21 March 1918, the RFC, hoping to confuse the enemy, ordered all single-seat fighter squadrons to change their unit markings, while all two-seater units – including the Bristol F2B squadrons – dispensed with them altogether, their only distinguishing features thereafter being the location, style and size of the letters or numerals that identified the individual aeroplane. In No 20 Sqn's case, the white letter was extraordinarily small and tucked inconspicuously below the pilot's cockpit.

'Maj E H Johnson, who commanded No 20 Sqn in 1918 in France, considered, I believe quite rightly, that bizarre markings would probably deter engagement when recognised as the Bristol Fighters of No 20 Sqn', recalled Stanley L Walters, a South African, who flew with the unit in the

Among the many FE 2d crewmen who moved on to Bristol F 2Bs with No 20 Sqn was Lt Albert Edward Woodbridge, an observer whose four Albatros D Vs claimed on 6 July 1917 included that of Manfred von Richthofen, wounded in the head. He added three more enemy aeroplanes to his tally in F 2Bs between 17 October and 8 November, with 2Lt William Durrand as his pilot (*Norman Franks*)

latter half of that year. 'This sounds, and possibly was, a bit arrogant. Reverting to the letter given each aircraft in No 20 Sqn, we paid little attention to them, as log book entries will indicate. Serial numbers were always used when referring to a particular aircraft'.

Formed at Netheravon on 1 September 1915, No 20 Sqn was equipped with FE 2bs when it commenced operations from Clairmarais, in France, in February 1916, switching to FE 2ds by July. In spite of their clumsy appearance, No 20 Sqn proved its 'Fees' to be anything but helpless, being credited with 203 victories.

When FE 2d A39 was downed in flames by Vzfw Walter Göttsch of *Jasta* 8 on 7 January 1917, its pilot, Sgt Thomas T Mottershead, brought the burning aeroplane, and observer Lt W E Gower, back to Allied lines before it collapsed on landing three miles north of Bailleul. Mottershead, who died of his injuries on the 12th, received a posthumous VC.

Among three enemy aeroplanes claimed by FE 2d crews of No 20 Sqn on 5 June 1917, that downed by Lt Harold Leslie Satchell and 2Lt Thomas Archibald Mitford Stewart Lewis ended the life of Ltn Karl Emil Schäfer, a 30-victory ace of von Richthofen's *Jasta* 11, then commanding *Jasta* 28. Moreover, while the squadron's claim of ten Albatros on 6 July (four of which were credited to Lt Douglas Charles Cunnell and 2Lt Albert Edward Woodbridge) was grotesquely exaggerated, the team did score a legitimate success in driving down the enemy leader – none other than *Rittmeister* Manfred von Richthofen himself – with a head wound that put him out of the war for weeks.

Such was the foundation established by No 20 Sqn's 'Fees' when it exchanged the last of them for Bristol F 2Bs in August 1917. The first 'Biff' victory for the unit was scored on 3 September by Lts Reginald Milburn Makepeace and Melville Wells Waddington in A7214 when they sent an Albatros D V crashing between Menin and Werwicq.

Born in Liverpool on 27 December 1887, Makepeace was a Canadian resident when war broke out in 1914. Posted to No 20 Sqn on 8 June 1917, he had scored his first eight victories in FE 2ds, while the 21-year-old, Toronto-born, Waddington, a former member of the Canadian Field Artillery, had seven previous victories in 'Fees'. The two continued to score thereafter, with an Albatros on 5 September, one on the 11th and two on 17 October. Makepeace had claimed three more by 4 January 1918, then was promoted to captain, transferred to No 11 Sqn on 23 January and scored his 17th, and final, victory (over a DFW C V) five days later – not as a pilot, but as observer to future 16-victory ace 2Lt John Stanley Chick. After all the combat he had seen, Makepeace was killed in a flying accident at Turnberry, in Ayrshire, on 28 May 1918.

2Lt William Durrand had previously been credited with four enemy aeroplanes piloting FE 2ds when he switched to the Bristol, and with Sgt William Joseph Benger from Ewell, Surrey, as his observer, shot an Albatros D V down in flames over Moorslede on 27 September. On 17 October he destroyed a DFW C V in concert with 2Lt Albert Woodbridge, who would also occupy Durrand's rear cockpit for the destruction of Albatros D Vs on 27 October and 8 November. After the war Woodbridge became a pilot, and following a spell in civil aviation, rejoined the RAF. However, while serving in the Middle East he was killed when the mail aeroplane in which he was attempting a night landing crashed at Jask, in Persia, on 7 September 1929.

On 9 September Lt Harry George Ernest Luchford, with Lt Richard Frank Hill in the observer's pit, drove an Albatros down out of control near Becelaere. It was the 12th victory for 23-year-old Harry Luchford, a former bank clerk from Bromley, in Kent, with previous service in the Norfolk Regiment, the Army Service Corps and the Indian Cavalry Division, prior to joining the RFC in January 1916. After qualifying as a pilot in May of that year, he joined No 20 Sqn that same month and was credited with 11 victories flying FE 2ds.

A pre-war bank clerk from Bromley, Kent, Lt Henry George Ernest Luchford was credited with 11 victories in FE 2ds and another 13 in Bristol F 2Bs with No 20 Sqn, also receiving the MC and Bar. His fortunes ran out on 2 December 1917, when he was shot down and killed near Becelaere by Ltn Walter von Bülow of *Jasta* 36. His observer, Capt J E Johnston, survived to become a PoW (*Norman Franks*)

Richard Hill, born at Jarvis Bank in Crowborough, Sussex, on 28 April 1899, was a student at Charterhouse School in Weekites until April 1917, when he left to join the RFC and, after receiving his commission, was duly assigned to No 20 Sqn in July. He scored his first victory while serving as observer to 2Lt C B Simpson on 19 August.

Luchford and Hill continued to score throughout September, with Albatros D Vs on the 11th, 21st and 25th, and a double victory over Menin on the 28th, although that last combat was costly for the squadron – 2Lts H F Tomlin and H T Noble, and Capt J S Campbell and Driver G Tester being shot down by Oblt Harald Auffahrth and Ltn Josef Veltjens of *Jasta* 18. After destroying one more Albatros on 1 October, Luchford and Hill were both awarded the MC, but Hill was withdrawn to England at the end of the month for training duties. Richard Hill later developed appendicitis, and after two operations, died on 17 September 1918.

Born in Oldham on 26 December 1896, Cpl Frank Johnson was credited with four enemy aeroplanes destroyed and earned the DCM as an observer in FE 2bs with No 22 Sqn. He then trained as a pilot and returned to combat flying Bristols with No 20 Sqn, adding nine victories between 11 October 1917 and 17 February 1918. Sgt Johnson then transferred to No 62 Sqn, raised his total to 16 with an enemy aeroplane on 27 March 1918 and two Albatros D Vs on 12 April, and got a Bar to his DCM the following month (*Norman Franks*)

Luchford's next success was over two Albatros D Vs on 11 October, with Sgt Benger, these bringing the latter's score up to five and earning him the Military Medal. On 17 October Luchford teamed with Lt Victor Rodney Stokes White, who had scored his first victory in a 1½ Strutter of No 45 Sqn before joining No 20 Sqn, to destroy an Albatros over Dadizeele. However, in the

Lt Victor Rodney Stokes White scored his first victory as an observer in a Sopwith 1½ Strutter of No 45 Sqn, later adding six more with No 20 Sqn, including four between 17 and 21 October 1917 in Bristol F 2B B1138, with Capt H G E Luchford as his pilot (*Norman Franks*)

Lt Henry George Crowe (left), a No 20 Sqn observer from Donnybrook, in Dublin, shared five of his eight victories with 2Lt Douglas Graham Cooke (right), and in April 1918 he survived being shot down six times in eleven days! Nine of Cooke's 13 victories were scored using his front gun (*Norman Franks*)

same engagement the unit suffered the loss of Benger and his pilot, Capt Arthur Gilbert Vivian Taylor, a former Indian Army infantryman with three FE 2d and four Bristol Fighter victories to his credit, killed over Poelcapelle by Ltn Theodor Quandt of *Jasta* 36. Luchford and White destroyed an Albatros D V and a DFW C V the next day. An LVG on the 21st brought Luchford's total to 24 and White's to six.

'Canadian' Ace

Another of No 20 Sqn's 'Canadians', 2Lt Wilfred Beaver was in fact an Englishman, born in Kingswood, Bristol, on 10 May 1897, but sent to Montreal in 1914 to live with an uncle and study dentistry. By the time he arrived there on 4 August, Britain was at war, and on the 7th he enlisted in the 1st Canadian Home Battalion. In 1915, Beaver initially served with the Royal Canadian Field Artillery in France, but on 28 February 1917 he joined the RFC. Following flight training he joined No 20 Sqn at St Marie Capelle on 22 October. After five practice flights Beaver went on his first patrol on the 29th, and the next day he had his first run-in with the enemy between Ypres and Passchendaele, resulting in his observer, Pvte C M Snoulton, being wounded.

On 13 November Beaver scored his first victory – a D V destroyed southeast of the Houthulst Forest. His observer on that occasion was 2Lt Cyril John Agelasto, a 20-year-old from West Hampstead with previous service in Nos 59 and 43 Sqns, and credited with an Albatros D V while in a Sopwith 1 1/2 Strutter with the latter unit on 29 July. Later teamed up with Canadian 2Lt David McKay McGoun (9 victories) and 2Lt Douglas Graham Cooke (13), Agelasto would survive the war as a full lieutenant with nine victories to his credit.

Assigned Bristol F 2B B883, Beaver teamed with AM M N Mather to destroy an Albatros southeast of Passchendaele on 2 December, but No 20 Sqn would end the day in mourning as Harry Luchford was mortally wounded and his observer, Capt J E Johnston, taken prisoner by Ltn Walter von Bülow of *Jasta* 36. After one more success on 5 December, Mather would raise his tally to eight with other pilots, while Beaver downed two-seaters on 3 and 6 January 1918 with 2Lt H E Easton, a former member of the 9th Battalion, London Regiment, from Brondesbury Park, northeast London, as his observer. Changing over to F 2B B1156, Beaver and Easton downed D Vs over Roulers on 3 and 4 February, and two on the 5th. A two-seater on 16 February and an Albatros on 23 March completed their collaboration – three days later Easton was injured and invalided out of the squadron.

Born in Bristol in 1897, Capt Wilfred Beaver had just arrived in Montreal, Canada, when war broke out, and he swiftly joined up. Flying F 2Bs in No 20 Sqn, he was credited with 19 victories before being wounded on 13 June 1918. Seeking employment opportunites postwar in the United States, he became an American citizen in 1926 (*Steve St Martin Collection via Greg VanWyngarden*)

Promoted to first lieutenant on 4 April, Beaver went on to be one of seven Bristol pilots to surpass Reginald Makepeace's score in No 20 Sqn. The most successful, Dennis Latimer, hailed from Dublin,

Ireland, and joined the unit early in 1918. His first victory, over an Albatros on 13 March, was also the second for his observer, 2Lt John J Scaramanga, who subsequently went on to acedom and death with No 22 Sqn. Latimer's next, an Albatros out of control on 21 April, was the third for 20-year-old Lt Tom Cecil Noel, a resident of Oakham, Rutland, who had been a student at Eton College before the war and an officer with the 3rd King's Own Scottish Borderers – a veteran of trench warfare, he had already been awarded the MC prior to joining the RFC.

On 25 April Beaver and Mather downed an Albatros in flames north of Ploegsteert Woods, probably wounding Ltn Alfred King of *Jasta* 40. Coincidentally, on that same day two more American volunteers arrived at No 20 Sqn's aerodrome at Boisdinghem. The sons of Auguste Florian Jaccaci, an expatriate Frenchman of Hungarian descent, and Mabel Thomas Thayer, the daughter of a Hingham, Massachusetts, minister, Paul Thayer Iaccaci had been born in Paris on 26 July 1890 and August Thayer Iaccaci in Hingham on 6 June 1893.

While they were still children, the Iaccacis' parents underwent a rancorous separation that resulted in August (or Thayer, as he preferred to be called) studying in England and Switzerland under his father's aegis, while Paul stayed with his mother, studying in Nolan's School at Cambridge, Massachusetts. Thayer later returned to the United States and entered Princeton University, where he excelled in athletics, hockey and swimming. Paul spent two years at Harvard before leaving to support his mother as a businessman and a banker.

Joining Company I, 7th Regiment, New York National Guard, both Iaccaci brothers served along the Mexican border in 1916, but after returning to New York they headed north to Toronto in February 1917 and enlisted in the RFC, in spite of Thayer's faulty eyesight. After training in Canada, they shipped out to France on 30 March 1918, across the Channel on 3 April and on to No 20 Sqn three weeks later.

RETURN OF AN ACE

April 1918 also saw one of the pioneer F 2A pilots return to combat as a captain and flight leader in No 20 Sqn. Born in Kew Gardens, London, on 10 May 1893, Thomas P Middleton had previously scored seven victories with No 48 Sqn. His observer of choice, Capt Frank Godfrey, had been born in Godalming, Surrey, on 16 August 1889, and after working as an accountant and assistant secretary to Alderman E Bridger in his home town, had served in the 19th Battalion of the Middlesex Regiment and Public Works Pioneers, before joining the RFC and being assigned to No 20 Sqn on 3 March.

Middleton and Godfrey started off by shooting down two Albatros D Vs on 17 April, followed by two more on 3 May, the latter date also seeing Beaver, with Capt N W Taylor as his observer, add an Albatros to his tally as well.

May proved to be a busy, productive month for several of No 20 Sqn's leading aces. Middleton and Godfrey accounted for one Albatros and one triplane on the morning of the 8th, while Latimer and Noel were credited with an Albatros D V and a Fokker Dr I in flames and two triplanes out of control that afternoon. Another triplane in flames at 1645 hrs became the first victory for Lt Victor Groom and 2Lt Ernest Hardcastle.

Lt Victor E Groom and 2Lt Ernest Hardcastle of No 20 Sqn sit in Bristol F 2B D7939 'P' at Boisdinghem aerodrome in early August 1918. Bill Thomson claimed that he often flew this aeroplane, appropriately marked with the legend *"Toronto"*, but he was credited with no victories in it, whereas Groom and Hardcastle scored two on 31 July (*Jack Eder*)

Capt John Herbert Hedley was an observer ace of No 20 Sqn, being credited with 11 victories between 3 December 1917 and 23 March 1918, for which he was gazetted for the French *Croix de Guerre*, before he and Capt R K Kirkman were shot down south of Albert and taken prisoner in Bristol B1156. Much was made of their being victims of Manfred von Richthofen, but his 'Bristol' claim (possibly an Armstrong Whitworth FK 8) was made hours later, their more likely victor being Ltn Karl Gallwitz of *Jasta* Boelcke (*Norman Franks*)

Born in Peckham, southeast London, on 4 August 1898, Victor Emmanuel Groom had joined the Artists Rifles and was commissioned in the West Yorkshire Regiment in April 1917. In September he joined the RFC and arrived at No 20 Sqn on 18 March 1918. One of Groom's first patrols was almost his last when a Very light fired by his flight leader fell into his observer's cockpit and ignited a pouch full of flares and cartridges. His observer put out the fire, but burned his hands in the process.

Groom's most frequent teammate, Ernest Hardcastle, was born on 31 December 1898 in Dudley Hill, Bradford, and had worked for the Bradford Chamber of Commerce before the war. After serving in the King's Own Yorkshire Rifles, Hardcastle transferred to the RFC in August 1917, and on 18 April 1918 steamed to France and was assigned to No 20 Sqn as an observer.

On 9 May an Albatros was destroyed by now-Capt Beaver and 28-year-old Sgt Ernest Arthur Deighton, from Masham, Yorkshire, while another Albatros destroyed opened the accounts of Canadian Lt William McKenzie Thomson and 2Lt George Hubert Kemp. Born in Lachine, Quebec, on 15 September 1898, Bill Thomson had been raised and educated in Toronto. On 14 May he and Kemp, who came from Charlton, in southeast London, scored again between Werwicq and Zillebeke, killing Ltn Erich Weiss of *Jasta* 33. Latimer and Noel also downed two Albatros that day, with Uffz Friedrich Karl Florian of *Jasta* 51 being taken prisoner, while Groom and Hardcastle destroyed a D V and a two-seater. Latimer and Noel downed a Pfalz and a Dr I on the 17th, and two more D Vs fell to Thomson and Kemp that same day.

On 18 May Latimer and Noel downed three Pfalz D IIIs, and two of the squadron's Americans also opened their accounts as Lt Paul Iaccaci

Lt Bill Thomson stands beside F 2B A7278 while 2Lt George Hubert Kemp poses in the observer's pit at St Marie Capelle in March 1918. Kemp scored all 12 of his victories with Thomson as his pilot, although none were achieved in A7278. After participating in the destruction of two Albatros D Vs, Kemp was killed in action on 1 June 1918 (*Norman Franks*)

and his observer, 32-year-old 1AM Arthur Newland from Enfield-Washington, drove a Fokker Dr I down out of control southwest of Nieppe, while Thomson and Kemp sent a Pfalz down out of control south of Merville. Groom and Hardcastle drove an Albatros D V down out of control at 1030 hrs the next day, while Lt Thayer Iaccaci teamed up with Newland to destroy a Pfalz at 1040 hrs. Thomson and Kemp destroyed another at 1045 hrs and Paul Iaccaci, with Sgt W Sansome in the observer's pit, destroyed a triplane ten minutes later.

Middleton teamed with Lt Alfred Mills, a 20-year-old graduate of Campbell College, Belfast, to destroy an enemy two-seater on 22 May, while Thayer Iaccaci and Newland eliminated another, and Thomson, flying with Lt C G Gass as his observer, drove a D V down out of control. Flight teamwork came into play on the 27th, as Beaver used his front gun to send a D V down in flames, his observer, Deighton, downed two triplanes and Thayer Iaccaci and Newland destroyed a Pfalz. Thomson and Gass downed a D V, Beaver and Deighton destroyed a triplane and Middleton and Mills also got a D V on the 29th, the latter team duly accounting for an Albatros and a Pfalz the next day.

The last day of May was a particularly active one for No 20 Sqn's aces. During a morning scrap southwest of Armentières, Middleton and Mills destroyed a Pfalz at 0740 hrs and Thayer Iaccaci and Sgt D A Malpas downed an Albatros 15 minutes later. At about that same time Paul Iaccaci and Newland destroyed two Albatros, one in flames, near Merville. During the afternoon patrol, Thayer Iaccaci, with Hardcastle as his observer, drove a Pfalz down out of control at 1850 hrs, while Paul Iaccaci, now flying with 1AM S W Melbourne, did the same to a D V.

The daily encounters continued without missing a beat on 1 June, as a morning patrol of No 20 Sqn Bristols got into a spirited fight with 25 Pfalz D IIIs north of Comines. Enemy aeroplanes fell to the teams of Latimer and Noel and Thayer Iaccaci and Sgt W O'Neill north of Merville, while Groom and Hardcastle and Thomson and Kemp each scored double victories. Possible victims were Vzfw Friedrich Neumann of *Jasta* 37, killed between Etinham and Péronne, and Uffz Kroeger of *Jasta* 7, wounded.

Sgt Ernest A Deighton manned the rear Lewis for six of Wilfred Beaver's victories, as well as three of Lt Leslie Howard Tandy Capel's seven, four of Lt David John Weston's 13, and in Lt Ernest H Lindup's fifth. Injured on 15 July, Deighton was awarded the DCM and had a personal tally of 15 (*Norman Franks*)

On the debit side, two Bristols were driven down in Allied lines and credited to Ltn Josef Jacobs of *Jasta* 7 and Ltn Albert Hets of *Jasta* 37. Lt Thomas Cathcart Traill and his Welsh observer, 2Lt Percy Griffith Jones, were unhurt and would go on to score eight and five victories, respectively. Bill Thomson also survived uninjured but Kemp, whose score then stood at 12, was killed. He was subsequently buried at Longuenesse Souvenir Cemetery at St Omer.

Thayer Iaccaci and Newland downed a Pfalz on 8 June, while Middleton and Godfrey got two more. Thomson and 25-year-old 2Lt Francis James Ralph from Turlanton, in Leicester, who had been a draughtsman with the Co-op Gas Company before he enlisted in

1915, destroyed a Pfalz the next day. Middleton and Godfrey claimed another Pfalz on the 12th.

Beaver was leading 12 Bristols on a bombing run on 13 June when they were jumped by Albatros D Vas northwest of Armentières. A bullet penetrated Beaver's shoulder and lower neck, but he and Deighton managed to drive a D V down out of control before heading back to base, while Paul Iaccaci and Noble also claimed an Albatros out of control.

Awarded the MC by King George V, promoted to captain and credited with 19 victories, Wilfred Beaver emigrated to the United States after the war, became a naturalised American citizen on 20 September 1926 and served in the Eighth Air Force during World War 2, retiring from the USAF as a colonel in 1955. He died of heart failure in West Point, Mississippi, on 21 August 1986.

Ernest Deighton, who had been awarded the DCM on 7 June, flew on with Lt Leslie Howard Tandy Capel as his pilot, downing two Pfalz D IIIs on the 17th and one on the 23rd to bring his score up to 15, and Capel's to seven. Deighton finally returned to England after being slightly injured on 15 July, dying in Bournemouth, Hampshire, on 5 December 1957.

A Pfalz went down to each of the Iaccacis and their gunners, Noble and Newland, near Houthem on 17 June, while another Pfalz was destroyed by Groom and Hardcastle and a Fokker D VII fell to Thomson and his observer, Sgt J D C Summers. Paul Iaccaci and 2Lt Ralphs downed another out of control on the 26th.

On the last day of June Thayer Iaccaci and Newland claimed a Pfalz and Capt Horace Percy Lale finally became an ace when he and Ernest Hardcastle destroyed a Fokker D VII southwest of Menin. Born in Sherwood, Nottinghamshire, on 8 April 1896, Lale had joined the RFC in 1916, and like Middleton, had cut his teeth on No 48 Sqn's Bristols, scoring four victories between 24 June and 14 September 1917. After a period of home defence in No 39 Sqn, he returned to the Western Front as a flight leader in No 20 Sqn.

Latimer and Noel downed a triplane on 1 July. The next day Weston and Noble claimed a Pfalz, and a Fokker fell to USAS pilot 1Lt Earl W Sweeney and 2Lt Clement Graham Boothroyd, who had been born in Jesmond, Newcastle-on-Tyne, on 25 August 1899, but lived in Halifax, Yorkshire, when war broke out. The flight paid a stiff price, however, losing two Bristols with their crews killed, and a third shot up and its observer, 2Lt P G Jones, also killed at the hands of Ltn Josef Schäfer of *Jasta* 16b and Ltn Dieter Collin and Vzfw Franz Piechulek of *Jasta* 56.

Paul Iaccaci celebrated his country's 'Fourth of July' with an English observer, as he and 2Lt Ronald William Turner, a 20-year-old former carpenter-joiner from York, claimed three Albatros, followed by two Fokkers on the 10th. The only July success for Thayer Iaccaci – with Turner as his observer – was a Fokker shared with Latimer and Noel on the 14th. Turner, then credited with six victories, was awarded the DFC for his performance up to that time, but he was not finished.

Thomson and Ralphs shared in the destruction of a D VII with Latimer and Noel on 17 July. Turner, with Lt John Henry Colbert – who had been his pilot when he scored his first victory on 18 May – destroyed a Fokker north of Comines on the 24th, which along with two others probably accounted for the deaths of Uffz Kurt Hollemann and Vzfw

Born in Lachine, Quebec, but raised in Toronto, Lt William McKenzie Thomson became No 20 Sqn's second-ranking ace with 26 victories (*William McKenzie Thomson via Stuart W Taylor*)

Capt Horace Percy Lale, standing between Lts Kirby and Salcer of No 20 Sqn, had scored four previous victories with No 48 Sqn between 24 June and 14 September 1917, raising his total to 23 by 30 October 1918 (*Norman Franks*)

Lts William H Thomson and Victor Emmanuel Groom of No 20 Sqn (*Norman Franks*)

Kurt Beineck of *Jasta* 51, albeit at the price of a Bristol shot down by their commander, Oblt Hans-Eberhardt Gandert, observer Sgt M S Samson being killed and pilot Sgt H D Aldridge taken prisoner.

Contributing to five claims on the 25th, Lale and Ralphs destroyed a D VII and shared in downing another in flames, but 2Lt F J Shearer and Sgt D Malpas were killed by Ltn Friedrich Röth, commander of *Jasta* 16b. Among four Fokkers claimed on the 29th, one went to Middleton and Godfrey, another was credited to Colbert and Turner as the pilot's fifth and his observer's ninth overall, and one was driven down out of control by Sgt John J Cowell and Cpl Charles William Hill.

Cowell, an Irishman from Country Limerick, had previously shot down 15 Germans as an observer in FE 2ds, this success earning him the DCM, MM and Bar. After downing two Albatros D Vs out of control on 28 July 1917, he had departed No 20 Sqn to train as a pilot, then returned to his own unit to resume his scoring one year to the day since his last success.

30 July got off to an unfortunate start, with USAS pilot 1Lt Gregory H Zellers and his observer Sgt J D Cormack being killed over Mount Kemmel by Vzfw Piechulek of *Jasta* 56 at 0845 hrs. The squadron got some revenge in a large dogfight at 1930 hrs, claiming six Fokkers, including two in flames over Bailleul by Groom and Hardcastle, one crashing northeast of Bailleul by Thayer Iaccaci and 2Lt Harold Edwards, one to Lt W H Shell and Sgt J D C Summers, and one to Lt John Metcalfe Purcell and 2Lt John Hills. One of Groom's and Hardcastle's victims was probably Uffz Wilhelm Meyer of *Jasta* 16b, who came down badly wounded near Ypres, but No 20 Sqn lost Cowell and Hill, killed south of Ypres by Fritz Röth.

July ended on one more blue note for No 20 Sqn the next day, as Shell and Summers were brought down at Vieux Berquin by Oblt Auffarth of *Jasta* 29 and taken prisoner.

COUNTEROFFENSIVE

8 August 1918 marked the start of the great Amiens counteroffensive, starting the British Army on an advance that would prove irreversible. 'Every so often the squadron moved forward to a new aerodrome made by Chinese work battalions', Thayer Iaccaci observed, adding, 'The Hun seemed to get stronger in the air as they weakened on the ground. Their new Fokker D VII was a terribly good fighting aeroplane. The dogfights often had 25-30 aeroplanes in a single battle'.

The first aerial contribution No 20 Sqn made to the 'big push' did not come until 11 August, when Lale and Hills burned an observation balloon northwest of Courtrai and Sweeney and Boothroyd eliminated another south of Heule. A welter of activity began at 1800 hrs on 14 August, when Lale and Ralph downed a Fokker north of Menin, while Lts George Ebben Randall from London and George Victor Learmond from Glasgow – who had previously scored on 24 July – drove a Pfalz down out of control.

At 1830 hrs Thomson and his new observer, Lt M A McKenzie, attacked a two-seater between Dadizeele and Menin and forced it down out of control, then destroyed a Fokker, while Latimer and Newland disposed of two Pfalz D IIIas. The squadron lost another observer acc,

Personnel of No 20 Sqn at Boidinghem in early August 1918. From left to right are Lt Clement Graham Boothroyd (12 victories), 2Lt Ernest Hardcastle (12), Lt David Esplin Smith (6, killed in action on 14 August 1918), Lt Victor E Groom (8) and 2Lt John Hills (7, PoW on 14 March 1918) (*Norman Franks*)

however, when Lt D E Smith and 2Lt John Hills – whose score then stood at seven – were shot down and killed near Werwicq by Ltn d R Schramm of *Jasta* 56. During a morning balloon strafe the next day, Thomson and McKenzie downed a Fokker near Becelaere at 0710 hrs, and Lt W H Markham burned a 'gasbag' west of Comines at 0735 hrs. Markham was wounded, but managed to bring his F 2B and his observer, 2Lt E S Harvey, safely home.

The next big fight occurred near northeast Gheluwe on the 21st, during which Lale and Ralph claimed three scouts and a share in a third, Latimer and Newland destroyed two Pfalz near Menin, and Colbert and Edwards claimed a Fokker. Randall and Newland got a Fokker the next day as well, but F 2B D7993 was shot down by Ltn Willi Nebgen of *Jasta* 7 – Capt Dennis Latimer, No 20 Sqn's highest-scoring pilot with 28 victories, was taken prisoner and Lt Tom Noel, then credited with 24, was killed and buried at Perth (China Wall) in Zillebeke.

On 26 August No 20 Sqn moved to Vignacourt to support the 5th Brigade as part of the 22nd Wing. In September Ernest Hardcastle was hospitalised and Victor Groom was sent home for a rest, only to come down with influenza. Both men were awarded the DFC for their actions of 1 June and 30 July 1918.

Recovering after the war, Groom served with No 111 Sqn in Egypt in 1919, and in 1920 he flew DH 9As in Iraq with No 55 Sqn, earning a bar to his DFC for landing and rescuing a downed crew under hostile fire on 5 May 1921. During World War 2 he commanded the Middle East Air Force, having attained the rank of air marshal, and was later knighted, before retiring to Putney, west London. Sir Victor Groom died in Surrey on 6 December 1990. Ernest Hardcastle, credited with 12 victories, left the RAF on 13 February 1919, but re-enlisted in 1940, serving at the night flying operation training unit at Cranfield, near Bedford, until 1945. Retiring to Bexhill, Sussex, in 1971, he died in November 1973.

For the remaining aircrews of No 20 Sqn, September 1918 would be a month of intense combat, significant rises in tally and, for some, the final reckoning. During a savage encounter over Havrincourt Wood at 1745 hrs on the 3rd, Fokkers fell to Paul Iaccaci and Mills, Lale and Ralph and Randall and Learmond, and five minutes later USAS pilot 1Lt Claire R Oberst downed two Pfalz D XIIs with the help of his 20-year-old observer, Lt Richard Gordon-Bennett. Lale's aeroplane was badly shot about and possibly credited to Ltn Friedrich Vollbracht of *Jasta* 5. Lale made it to Allied lines but Francis Ralph, whose score then stood at 13, had been killed. He was duly buried at Villers Bretonneux Cemetery.

Ltn Josef Mai of *Jasta* 5 claimed a 'DH 4' in the action, but was wounded in the upper left leg. His 'victim' may in fact have been another Bristol, although No 20 Sqn's only casualties were Lale's shot-up machine and dead observer, thus showing that the Germans, too, were capable of misperceptions in the heat of combat.

Three Fokkers claimed on the 5th included one for Randall and Learmond and one for Lale and his replacement observer, the experienced Harold Edwards. Seven more victories the next day included two more for Lale and Edwards, two for Thayer Iaccaci and Newland and two for Paul Iaccaci and Mills, to which Lale and Edwards added another Fokker on the 7th. The next day, Paul Iaccaci was promoted to captain and transferred to No 48 Sqn to serve as a flight commander, but he added no more successes to the 17 victories he had scored with No 20 Sqn. Although pressured to join the USAS, Thayer chose to stay with his RAF unit. 'We were having a hard time and a good many losses near the end', he said. 'When I left the squadron, there was not one man but Newland who was there when I arrived'.

15 September saw eight more Fokker claims, including two for Thomson and Edwards and two for Thayer Iaccaci and Newland, plus a Hannover CL IIIa destroyed by Capt Middleton and Lt Mills. Neither of the two enemy fighter units recorded losses, but claims by Oblt Hasso von Wedel of Royal Saxon *Jasta* 24 and Ltn Ulrich Neckel of *Jasta* 6 were matched by the F 2Bs of 2Lt A B D Campbell and Sgt T A Stac, and of 2Lts F E Finch and C G Russell, all of whom became PoWs. Additionally, observer Sgt A J Winch was wounded.

Moving up to Suzanne-sur-Somme on 16 September, No 20 Sqn added another seven to its tally, including a Fokker by Thayer Iaccaci and Newland, while Thomson and Edwards got two and shared a third with Lt A R Strachan and 2Lt D M Calderwood. Bill Thomson left the squadron shortly after with 26 enemy aeroplanes to his credit and a subsequent promotion to captain. He eventually passed away in Toronto on 9 July 1987.

Of ten Fokkers claimed on the 20th, one was credited to Thayer Iaccaci and Newland, two to Lt Frederick George Harlock and 18-year-old 2Lt Arthur Stuart Draisey, two to Middleton and Mills, two to South African 2Lt Stanley L Walters and Lt T W Kirkpatrick, and two to Lts Malcolm McCall and Boothroyd, but Strachan and Calderwood were killed by Oblt Otto Schmidt, commander of *Jasta* 5. Lt Nicholson Stuart Boulton, now teamed up with the veteran Edwards, downed three Fokkers on the 23rd, bringing the pilot's total to six.

On the Move

The squadron advanced again on 24 September, this time to Proyart, and also claimed four more Fokkers, including one to Australian-born former Royal Engineer Capt Geoffrey Herbert Hooper and 2Lt Edwards, and another to Traill and Gordon-Bennett. The next day saw three Fokkers credited to Hooper and Edwards, two to Harlock and Draisey and one each to Walters and Kirkpatrick, Traill and Gordon-Bennett and McCall and Boothroyd, but Gordon-Bennett was wounded and was transported to hospital in England in early October.

'Sometimes we would hit the enemy aircraft with front guns and finish him off with rear guns or vice versa', Thayer Iaccaci explained. 'One time, on 27 September, we got two enemy aircraft at once – one with the front guns and the other with the rear guns. My logbook shows mostly "we got

Members of No 20 Sqn relax between missions at Boisdinghem. They are, from left to right, Lt Clement G Boothroyd (with dog), Capt Thomas P Middleton (27), Lt Walter Noble, Lt Victor Groom and Capt Frank Godfrey (12 victories) (*Jack Eder*)

one" and not often "I got one" or "Newland got one"'.

In addition to his and Newland's double that day, McCall and Boothroyd and Harlock and Draisey each claimed a Fokker, but 2Lts F E Turner and C E Clark were killed by Offz Stv Friedrich Altemeier of *Jasta* 24s. Hooper and Edwards claimed three Fokkers, and single victories were credited to Walters and Kirkpatrick, McCall and Boothroyd, and Traill and Burbidge on the 29th, but Boulton and observer 2Lt C H Case were killed, also credited to Altemeier.

By October the German army was falling back, but the *Luftstreitkräfte* remained full of fight. Traill and Burbidge sent a Fokker down out of control on the 1st and Lale and Learmond did likewise on the 3rd, while Harlock and 2Lt J R Kidd destroyed another. The squadron moved up to Moislains on the 7th, and Hooper, with Lt M A McKenzie, sent a Fokker down out of control near Guise on the 18th.

Five more Fokkers were claimed on the 23rd, including two by Lale and Boothroyd, and one by Traill and Burbidge, but as the patrol returned Traill's aeroplane collided with another Bristol. The other Bristol's crewmen, 2Lt H L Fennal and Sgt C Aitken, were killed, and Traill's F 2B spun down with part of the right wing torn away. Burbidge courageously climbed out on the lower plane, using his body weight to counter the spin, allowing Traill to recover enough for a crash landing. Burbidge was hurled from the wreck and landed on his face, breaking his nose and biting through his tongue, but Traill was unhurt.

Credited with eight victories and awarded the DFC, Traill commanded No 14 Sqn in Amman after the war, and was commanding

Lts Stanley L Walters (pilot) and T W Kirkpatrick pose in F 2B F6121 after the armistice. The team was credited with four victories, but the South African Walters stated that none were scored in F6121 (*Jack Eder*)

No 19 Group, Coastal Command, when he retired with the rank of air vice-marshal in 1954.

The rapid Allied advance was reflected by another move to Iris Farm, near Elincourt, on the 25th, and Lale and Boothroyd claimed two of four Fokkers downed on the 30th, bringing the pilot's final score to 23 and Boothroyd's to 12.

There was to be no let up for No 20 Sqn in the last weeks of the war, Randall and Learmond downing a Fokker on 3 and 9 November. Their last two victories were scored on the 10th, thus taking Randall's tally to 11 and Learmond's to nine. These successes were among five claims made by the squadron, one also going to Hooper and McKenzie for the pilot's 11th overall. The unit also lost its last two aeroplanes that day, less than 24 hours before the armistice.

Horace Lale went on to earn a bar to his wartime DFC flying in Waziristan, in the North West Frontier, where he was also awarded the DSO in the spring of 1920 for 'personal gallantry and administrative efficiency'. He was given command of No 32 Sqn in 1924 and No 30 Sqn in 1928, rising to the rank of wing commander in 1930 and group captain in 1936. After returning to service in World War 2, Lale was active for several years on the Grant's Committee of the RAF Benevolent Fund before his death in the 1950s.

It is ironic how close war brought the Iaccaci brothers, even to their having identical scores of 17 and both receiving the DFC, for the postwar years drove them farther apart. The death of their father of a cerebral haemorrhage on 22 July 1930 only exacerbated the rift, as Thayer, who adopted his father's spelling of 'Jaccaci', was named the principal beneficiary in his will, inheriting a $200,000 estate, whereas Mabel received a life annuity of $1600 and Paul got nothing. Paul went on to be a successful banker and restaurant owner, while Thayer achieved prominence in the Eastman Kodak camera firm.

Some 20 years after the armistice, Thayer suffered a nervous breakdown, undoubtedly related to his wartime experiences. He eventually recovered, and in later years the estranged brothers reconciled their differences. On 26 July 1965, however, Paul Thayer Iaccaci died in Mary Hitchcock Hospital, Hanover, New Hampshire, of burns suffered in a heater explosion in his home. August Thayer Iaccaci died of natural causes in Madison, Connecticut, on 30 April 1980.

Brothers Capts August Thayer and Paul Thayer Iaccaci, photographed in late November 1918, had both scored 17 victories and earned DFCs in No 20 Sqn, but their lives would bitterly diverge in the postwar years (*Jack Eder*)

Members of No 20 Sqn take a break at Boisdinghem. They are, from left to right, Capt Dennis Latimer (30 victories), Lt Walter Noble (12), Lt Paul Thayer Iaccaci (17), unidentified and Capt Thomas Percy Middleton (27) (*Norman Franks*)

A FIGHTING EMPHASIS

The last two Bristol Fighter units to serve over the Western Front, Nos 62 and 88 Sqns, focused their activities primarily on air superiority, rather than reconnaissance, often serving as fighter escorts to formations of DH 4s and DH 9s on bombing missions. No 62 Sqn was formed in May 1917 and commenced operations from Serny aerodrome in February 1918.

An F 2B of No 62 Sqn, undergoing extensive repairs at Panques aerodrome, displays the squadron markings used by the unit until 22 March 1918 (*Greg VanWyngarden*)

First blood was drawn on the 17th when 22-year-old Capt Geoffrey Forrest Hughes from Sydney, New South Wales, and Capt Hugh Claye, a 27-year-old with pre-war service in the 5th Nottingham and Derby Regiment, Territorial Force, encountered two enemy aeroplanes and drove them back toward their lines. On the 21st, the same team opened their unit's account by sending a large two-seater down 200 yards behind German lines near Armentières. Moving up to Cachy on 1 March, No 62 Sqn claimed a D V destroyed and five out of control on 10 March – the former, and one of the out of controls, credited to Claye and Hughes – and two triplanes the next day, one of which again was credited to Claye and Hughes.

On 12 March 'The Cheery 62s' had their first run-in with the Red Baron's Circus. Two Bristols of the flight were diving on a German two-seater when observer 2Lt H J Sparks test-fired his Lewis gun and a cartridge fell between the pilot's stick and a metal fitting, jamming the controls. In his efforts to dislodge it, 2Lt C L F Clutterbuck lost altitude, and was promptly pounced on by *Rittmeister* Manfred von Richthofen. In short order both petrol tanks were shot through, Sparks wounded in the left arm and Clutterbuck compelled to land B1251 south of Nauroy.

Capt Geoffrey Forrest Hughes of No 62 Sqn shares a light moment with Lt Wilfred Beaver of No 20 Sqn (*Steve St Martin Collection via Norman Franks*)

Meanwhile, Ltn Werner Steinhäuser of *Jasta* 11 brought down Lt J H Ferguson and Sgt D Lough, who were captured. The outstanding performance on the German side, however, again came from the Baron's brother Lothar, an 'old hand' at vanquishing Bristols since their combat debut 11 months earlier. First shooting 'A' Flight leader's aeroplane down in flames over Maretz, killing Capt Douglas Stewart Kennedy MC and Lt Hugh Goddard Gill, Lothar then forced a second F 2B down at Clary, resulting in 2Lt O B Fenton and Lt H P Boyce becoming PoWs.

Although *Jasta* 11 recorded no losses in the massacre, No 62 Sqn credited a Dr I to Lts George Everard Gibbons and Sidney Arthur William

Knights, and an enemy aircraft to 2Lts Percy R Hampton and L C Lane. 'There were probably 25-30 engaged, so we had to look out for other enemy aircraft and collisions' recalled Hampton in 1972, also bearing witness to the loss of Kennedy;

'He was abreast of me about 50 yards to starboard when hit. The aircraft immediately burst into a large ball of flame and he and his observer, Lt Gill, jumped overboard, so I was able to report his certain death on my return.'

Lt Sidney Arthur William Knights (left) poses with pilot Capt George Everard Gibbons, with whom he scored all eight of his victories while in No 62 Sqn before being hospitalised on 10 July 1918. Gibbons went on to down nine more enemy aeroplanes with 2Lt Thomas Elliott as his observer (*Norman Franks*)

The day before his double victory at No 62 Sqn's expense, Lothar had driven one of No 48 Sqn's aeroplanes down in Allied lines, its lucky crew surviving unhurt. Three F 2Bs in two days boosted his total to 29 (eight of them Bristols), but on 13 March he would encounter one 'Biff' too many. That afternoon, Hughes and Claye led a flight of 11 Bristols on patrol at 16,000 ft over Le Cateau when they spotted ten Dr Is and ten Albatros D Vs below them. A flight of DH 4s was in the vicinity, so Hughes decided to draw the German fighters away from them. He succeeded in doing so, but also attracted the attention of five more triplanes and five Pfalz D IIIs.

'It was now five minutes after the time our patrol was due to land, and having succeeded in drawing all the enemy aircraft to a point just east of Cambrai, I considered our work was done, and turned for the lines not intending to be drawn into combat against at least 40 enemy aircraft', Hughes reported afterwards. 'As I turned to cross the lines, I saw one of my Bristols dive on the triplanes below us. Apparently another machine thought that it was I who had dived, for he followed the first. This blunder upset all my plans and I was forced to attack'.

Hughes drove a red and green triplane off one F 2B's tail, and then fired an 80-round burst at a second Dr I that was pursuing another Bristol, closing to ten yards until he saw the enemy pilot slump forward and go down out of control. Hughes then zoomed up and attacked a well-handled Dr I with a bright red nose. His observer, Claye, got a 50-round burst of Lewis into the triplane, which went down vertically with the top wing falling away in pieces.

Hughes and Claye were credited with the two Dr Is, while the teams of 2Lt S W Simonds and Sgt W N Holmes and Lts A R James and John Mathew Hay were each credited with Albatros D Vs out of control.

Bristol 'L' of No 62 Sqn at Planques in early March 1918 shows the squadron bands and typical letter placement for 'A' and 'C' Flights. 'B' Flight used numerals just forward of the fuselage roundel (*Greg VanWyngarden*)

Capt Geoffrey F Hughes is seen sat in F 2B C4630 of No 62 Sqn, decked out in full unit markings, at Planques in April 1918 (*Norman Franks*)

Another triplane and an Albatros also became the first victories for 2Lt William Ernest Staton and Horace Ernest Merritt. Those successes came at the cost of two Bristols, resulting in the death of a pilot, 2Lt Cyrus Allen, and the capture of 2Lt A B Well and G R Crammond, as well as Allen's observer, Lt N T Watson. *Jasta* 56 credited the two aeroplanes to Ltns Rudolf Heins and Franz Schlieff, but one of its pilots, Ltn Walter Bowien, was also killed.

Moreover, Ltn Lothar von Richthofen was wounded, either by the gunfire of Claye, Camel pilot Capt Augustus H Orlebar of No 73 Sqn, or both, and subsequently injured when his Dr I crash landed near Awoingt at 1030 hrs. It was the second of three wounds the Red Baron's brother would suffer in the course of the war, and it put him out of action for four months.

The next two months brought constant combat and a growing victory tally to No 62 Sqn, but its crews, including its most successful pilots and observers, frequently paid a high price. While escorting DH 4s on 19 May, for example, Lts Douglas Alfred Savage and E W Collis lost sight of their flight and came under attack by seven Albatros D Vas and two Pfalz D IIIas. Collis emptied a drum of Lewis into an Albatros that went down out of control over Bray before his gun jammed. Pursued by the two Pfalz while the Albatros stayed above, the Bristol's petrol tanks were shot through, but Savage managed to force land near Corbie – just 3000 yards on the Allied side of the lines. Theirs may have been an unconfirmed Bristol claimed by Ltn Fritz Pütter of *Jasta* 68.

Savage and Collis were fortunate, for elsewhere the rest of their flight was beset by more Germans, and although No 62 Sqn claimed another enemy aeroplane out of control – probably the Pfalz D IIIa in which Ltn Karl Bauernfeind of *Jasta* 34b crashed, suffering a skull fracture – they lost three more Bristols. Lt H C Hunter and Sgt J Lake were shot down by *Jasta* 34b's commander, Ltn Robert von Greim, Hunter being wounded and Lake killed. Lt Frank Atkinson was wounded and forced to land near Proyart, where he and his observer,

A more fortunate participant in the costly aerial melée of 19 May 1918 was Lt Douglas Alfred Savage, whose F 2B (B1336) was driven down in Allied lines, but not before he and his observer, Lt E W Collis, claimed an 'Albatros' out of control, which may in fact have been the Pfalz D IIIa in which Ltn Karl Bauernfeind of *Jasta* 34b crashed and was injured near Proyart. A Fokker Dr I driven down out of control on 2 June brought Savage's total to eight before he was posted home and awarded the MC (*Norman Franks*)

F 2B C4630, which accounted for 11 enemy aeroplanes as the mount of Capts Geoffrey F Hughes and Hugh Claye, was damaged and reconfigured with a long exhaust pipe. Its luck ran out with another pilot, Lt H A Clarke, in the cockpit on 19 May 1918, when it came down southwest of Hangest, Clarke and Claye being taken prisoner. Ltn August Delling of *Jasta* 34b claimed it, although the Germans credited the F 2B to anti-aircraft fire (*Greg VanWyngarden*)

Another of four Bristols lost by No 62 Sqn on 19 May was C4751 'T', in which 2Lt Frank Atkinson was wounded and brought down near Proyart by Vzfw Max Kahlow of *Jasta* 34b. Atkinson and his observer, Sgt Charles C Brammer, were taken prisoner. Elsewhere, Lt H C Hunter was brought down wounded and made a PoW, and his observer, Sgt J Lake, killed near Guillaucourt by *Jasta* 34b's commander, Oberltn Robert *Ritter* von Greim (*Greg VanWyngarden*)

Sgt Charles Brammer, were taken prisoner, probably victims of Vzfw Max Kahlow.

Lt H A Clarke and Capt Hugh Claye, in F 2B C4630, were attacked by Ltn August Delling of *Jasta* 34b and subsequently brought down and taken prisoner, but they were also claimed by a German flak unit and may also have been credited to Vzfw Otto Könnecke of *Jasta* 5 – in any case, not officially to Delling, who would nevertheless survive the war with six confirmed victories. Whatever the cause, in C4630 the Germans got their hands on both a Bristol and an observer that had accounted for 11 of their aeroplanes, although Claye's regular pilot, Hughes, was not present at the time to share their fate.

Geoffrey Hughes was awarded the Air Force Cross before returning to Australia, where he pursued a career in civil aviation. He died of pneumonia on 13 September 1951.

More Aces

In the months that followed, other Bristol teams advanced to the fore in No 62 Sqn. George Gibbons and Sidney Knights had downed a second enemy aeroplane on 17 March, and on the 21st Capt Thomas Laurence Purdom, a veteran of the King's Own Scottish Borderers who had flown BE 2s with No 15 Sqn throughout 1916, downed two Albatros D Vs to commence a fruitful collaboration with 2Lt Percival V C Chambers. The latter had been wounded four times with the 5th Battalion of the South Staffordshire Regiment before getting his commission on 28 March 1917 and joining No 62 Sqn as an observer on 28 December.

Lt John R Gordon, an observer with No 62 Sqn who was destined to achieve ace status, poses beside F 2B C4619 at Planques in early March 1918 (*Jack Eder*)

'Bull' Staton's claim of a Fokker Dr I downed in flames that same day marked the start of his partnership with Lt John Rutherford Gordon. Born in Gilberton, South Australia, on 18 June 1895, Gordon, then a sergeant in the 10th Battalion, Australian Imperial Force (AIF) had been in the first group to land at Gallipoli on 25 April 1915, getting a commission there on 4 August but subsequently being invalided home with typhoid. From the 74th Infantry, Gordon transferred into the Australian Flying Corps (AFC) and soloed in a Grahame-White at Point Cook on 6 April 1917. After departing for England on 16 June 1917, he became ill aboard ship and was declared medically unfit for AFC service. In January 1918, however, he was seconded as an observer to No 62 Sqn, and permanently assigned to 'A' Flight on 18 March.

Sgt Sorsby, one of those groundcrewmen essential to the aircrew's success, joins Lt John R Gordon and Capt William E Staton for a photo before F 2B C4619 after the squadron markings had been removed – much to the satisfaction of the aircrews, who did not like having so many prominent white bands around their cockpit area (*Greg VanWyngarden*)

Purdom and Chambers destroyed a D V in flames on 24 March, and claimed a double victory on the 26th, which Staton and Gordon outdid by despatching three that same day. Purdom and Chambers scored again on the 28th, Staton and Gordon got a D V on 1 April, and on 21 April both teams shared in the destruction of another Albatros southeast of Estaires.

The same two Bristol duos claimed an Albatros two-seater and a D V each on 3 May, while Gibbons and Knights downed two more D Vs. Purdom and Chambers downed a two-seater on 15 May, followed by a Fokker D VII and another two-seater two days later. Purdom's 13th, and final, victory (another D VII) was scored on the 19th with Sgt W N Holmes. Chambers, with 12 to his credit, was sent home with appendicitis on 26 June and left the RAF on 1 May 1919.

A former member of the King's Own Scottish Borderers and a BE 2 pilot of No 15 Sqn, Capt Thomas Laurence Purdom (left) scored 13 victories with No 62 Sqn between 21 March and 19 May 1918 – all but one shared with 2Lt Percival V G Chambers (right) (*Norman Franks*)

Staton and Gordon and Gibbons and Knights each added LVGs to their accounts on 22 May, and the latter pair eliminated a Fokker D VII and a Rumpler on the 28th, while Staton and Gordon downed two-seaters on 29 and 30 May.

June saw Staton and Gordon destroy a triplane on the 2nd, two Pfalz on the 5th and a Pfalz out of

In addition to being credited with 15 victories with No 62 Sqn, Wg Cdr John Rutherford Gordon could claim to have served in five air arms – the AFC, RFC, RAF, RAAF and RCAF – in the course of his long career (*Jack Eder*)

Capt William E 'Bull' Staton became No 62 Sqn's top-scorer with 26 victories before being wounded in September 1918 (*Norman Franks*)

control on the 8th. Of the 15 victories they had scored by the 17th, when Gordon departed to Home Establishment, Staton got eight, four were credited to his observer and three were joint successes (Gordon's observer's card credited him with five destroyed and two out of control).

Awarded the MC for his aerial victories and his participation in ground attack missions, Gordon returned to the AFC and qualified as a pilot just before the armistice, then travelled back to Australia on 6 May 1919. He became a committee member of the South Australia section of the Australian Aero Club when it was formed on 4 September 1919, and after a spell arranging buffalo shooting tours in the Northern Territory in 1931, he joined the staff of the Vacuum Oil Company in Adelaide in 1932. In World War 2 Gordon rejoined the RAAF, rising in rank from flight lieutenant to wing commander by 3 July 1945. Gordon died in Adelaide on 11 December 1978.

Staton resumed his scoring on 8 July with a Fokker Dr I, with Sgt W N Holmes (who was credited with eight victories with various pilots) as his observer. Gibbons, meanwhile, had lost Knights, who had been posted to the School of Aviation and later the Armament School back in England, but found a replacement in the person of 2Lt Thomas Elliott.

Born in Gateshead, County Durham, on 18 March 1898, Elliott had been a clerk with Raine and Company in Newcastle until his enlistment in April 1916, joining No 62 Sqn on 12 March 1918. His first victory was over an LVG, with 2Lt William Keith Swayze as his pilot, on 22 May, but he was subsequently assigned to Gibbons for what turned out to be the balance of their fighting careers. They were credited with enemy aircraft on 1 and 3 August and a two-seater on the 13th, then scored a succession of double victories over D VIIs on 22 August and on 3 and 4 September.

Elliott, who had scored an additional victory on 1 September when his pilot, Lt C Allday, suffered a gun jam and he shot the attacking D VII down in flames, was reassigned to instruct at No 1 School of Air Gunnery later that month. George Gibbons, 14 of whose 17 victories fell to his front gun, was awarded the MC, DFC and the French *Légion d'Honneur*. He died in Kingston, Surrey, on 13 October 1992.

Staton found a new regular observer in 2Lt Leslie Edwin Mitchell, a 24-year-old self-employed engineer from Leytonstone, Essex. They downed two aeroplanes on 12 August, a D VII the next day, and more Fokkers on 22 August and 3 and 4 September. Their best-documented victory came on 15 September, when they and SE 5a pilot 2Lt D E Cameron of No 1 Sqn brought down a Pfalz D XII at Marquion – in Allied lines – whose pilot, Ltn d R Paul Vogel of *Jasta* 23b, died of his wounds.

As No 62 Sqn was escorting DH 4s of No 57 Sqn back from a bombing attack on Beauvois aerodrome on 24 September, it came under attack by 30 Fokkers, three of which were claimed by observers of No 57 Sqn and one by Staton for his 26th victory. The Germans in turn claimed three Bristols, credited to Vzfw Robert Wirth of *Jasta* 37 and Ltns Lehmann and Fritz Jebens of *Jasta* 59. Wirth's victims, Lt N N Coope and 2Lt H S Mantle, were wounded and taken prisoner, but the two other F 2Bs came down in Allied lines. One was flown by Staton, who was severely wounded in the leg. Mitchell became observer to Lt L H O'Reilly, but on 29 September their Bristol – E2509 – was seen to break up and fall over Dury, probably the victim of an anti-aircraft shell.

Although unable to rejoin his unit before the armistice, Staton, who had ready been awarded the MC and DFC, got a Bar to his DFC on 6 October. He continued his career in the RAF, leading Whitleys of No 10 Sqn on some the first bombing raids on Germany after World War 2 broke out in September 1939, for which he was awarded the DSO the following year. Transferred to Singapore, Staton had the misfortune to be captured when the garrison surrendered to the Japanese in February 1942, and spent three years in true durance vile. He retired as an air vice marshal in 1952 and was subsequently made a Companion in the Order of the Bath.

In 1972 Staton was living in Emsworth, Hampshire, from whence he reported, 'I still fly. I live next door to an Air Station, and also fly with a light aeroplane club. I am the Commodore of the Emsworth Yacht Club and still sail racing dinghies – not bad for an old gaffer of 73'. William Staton passed away on 22 July 1983.

By the time of the armistice, No 62 Sqn had claimed 76 enemy aeroplanes destroyed and 85 out of control, ten of its pilots attaining ace status. The cost was high, however – 28 airmen killed in action and three in accidents, 32 taken prisoner, 22 wounded in action and 11 injured in accidents. In a remarkable comparison, the last Bristol unit to reach the Western Front, No 88 Sqn, claimed 147 enemy aeroplanes destroyed, but only lost two men killed, five wounded and ten missing.

A close-up of Staton and Gordon with C4619 reveals details of the cowling, propeller spinner and what seems to be an outline in the blue flight colour of 'C' Flight around the letter 'R' (*J R Gordon via Norman Franks*)

No 88 Sqn

Formed in Gosport in July 1917, No 88 Sqn moved to France in April 1918. In the course of its fighter-reconnaissance duties, the unit helped develop air-to-air wireless telegraphy, and like No 62 Sqn, participated in numerous bombing raids.

Three of the four pilots in the unit who achieved double-digit scores were 'colonials', two coming from Australia. Allan Hepburn was born in Melbourne, Victoria, on 11 October 1896, and had served in the Artists Rifles in France before joining the RFC and flying DH 5s with No 24 Sqn. While there, he met fellow Australian Edgar Charles Johnston, born in Perth, Western Australia, on 30 April 1896, and who had also seen action with the AIF in 1915-16, prior to learning to fly.

Hepburn was wounded on 26 October, but kept flying, and in mid-November was offered command of a flight in No 40 Sqn, succeeding Capt Edward V 'Mick' Mannock. Hepburn was injured in an accident shortly after his arrival, however, and upon recovery in England in April 1918, he was offered another command – 'A' Flight in newly formed No 88 Sqn. Coincidentally, Johnston, who had driven a D V out of control on 10 December 1917 – a feat not to be taken lightly when done in a DH 5 – was also posted to No 88 Sqn and given command of 'B' Flight.

Members of No 88 Sqn, identified as (from left to right) Lt Jack Marshall, Lt Dion, Lt H C Foley, 2Lt Vivian Voss, Lt W B Clarke and Lt James Gage (*Jack Eder*)

Capt Allan Hepburn DFC scored all 16 of his victories in F 2B C821 of No 88 Sqn, prior to receiving the much-photographed E4442, in which he got none (*Norman Franks*)

A dancer in his native Ontario before the war, Lt Kenneth B Conn became the leading ace of No 88 Sqn with 20 victories (*Norman Franks*)

Hepburn, with 2Lt G W Lambert as his observer, opened his account with an Albatros out of control on 17 May. Johnston resumed his scoring the next day by downing two D Vs – one in flames – north of Langemarck, aided by 19-year-old 2Lt John Rudkin from Grantham, Lincolnshire, who had served, and obtained his commission, in the 4th Reserve Dragoon Regiment before joining No 88 Sqn in April.

Hepburn's second success (an Albatros D V out of control over Ostend on 31 May) was achieved with 31-year-old 2AM Thomas Proctor from Belfast as his observer. The two claimed another D V in flames between Middelkerke and Ostend at 1935 hrs on 2 June, their victim possibly being Flg Horst Sawatzky of *Marine Feld Jasta* I, who came down wounded between Middelkerke and Nieuport at 2100 hrs (daylight savings time, as practised by the Germans, hence the discrepancy with the Allied time) in Albatros D V 4635/17.

Proctor went on to score two victories with Lt A R Stedman on 11 August and downed a Dr I flying with Lt Alec Williamson on the 19th (the latter's seventh of nine victories).

UNLIKELY ACE

The status of No 88 Sqn's leading ace was to be held by an unlikely seeming warrior. Born in Ashton, Ontario, on 11 July 1896, Kenneth Burns Conn was a dancer before the war. Joining the 3rd Reserve Battalion in 1915, he served in the 234th Battalion, CEF, in 1916, but transferred to the RFC in March 1917.

The observer who figured most frequently in Conn's subsequent combats, 2Lt Bruce Digby-Worsley, had been born in Tunbridge Wells, Kent, on 8 February 1896, and was a married man with previous service in the 5th Gloucestershire and 16th Middlesex regiments and the 5th King's Own Surrey Borderers between May 1915 and August 1917. Joining the RFC and obtaining an officer's commission on 3 January 1918, he returned to France with No 88 Sqn that April. Conn's partnership with Digby-Worsley got seriously under way when they destroyed two Albatros D Vs over Messines on 5 June.

Conn's next few successes involved Lt Bertram Hutchinson Smyth, who had been working in Argentina as a statistics clerk with the Buenos Aires Pacific Railway from May 1912 to February 1916, when he travelled to England and joined the 10th Battalion of the Gloucesters. Transferring to the RFC in February 1918 and joining No 88 Sqn on 16 April, he was in Conn's back seat on 28 June when the duo engaged a Halberstadt two-seater over the Houthulst Forest and shot it down in flames, killing Ltn d R Alfred Knödgen and Ltn Max Handschuher of *Fl.Abt.(A)* 288b.

The next day, they destroyed a Fokker D VII and shared in the destruction of another. In the same action, Capt K R Simpson and his observer, 19-year-old Sgt Charles Hill from Huddersfield, claimed another Fokker, but were themselves brought down southeast of Dixmuide and credited as the fifth victory for Flg Alexander Zenses of *Marine Feld Jasta* II, although the British made it to their lines unhurt. Similarly, 2Lt Robert James Cullen and his observer, 2Lt Edward Henry Ward, claimed three opponents, bringing both their scores up to five, before being shot down over Pervyse as victory No 16 for MFJ II's

Staffelführer, Ltn Theo Osterkamp – and again the wounded Cullen was able to nurse his Bristol and his observer to the safety of Allied lines.

Reverting to Digby-Worsley, Conn added two more D VIIs to his growing tally on 1 July, as did Johnston and Rudkin. Hepburn resumed his scoring by downing a Fokker D VII on 29 and 31 July with 19-year-old Sgt Ernest Antcliffe, a former private in the 270th Infantry Battalion, as his observer.

Johnston and Rudkin opened No 88 Sqn's contribution to the great Amiens offensive of 8 August with two Fokker Dr Is. The team downed two Fokker D VIIs on the 11th, only to be outdone by Lt Charles Findlay, a 27-year-old art student from Glasgow, and Digby-Worsley, who were credited with two crashed and two in flames, followed by another the next day. Johnston and Rudkin teamed up with Conn and Smyth to bring down a D VII on the 13th. On the 19th Conn and Smyth sent a D VII down out of control over Oignies and shared another with Johnston and Rudkin. Hepburn and 2Lt Horace George Eldon, a former laboratory assistant from Dorset, drove a D VII down out of control on the 29th.

Hepburn and Antcliffe opened September by destroying a Fokker D VII in flames east of Becelaere on the 1st. When No 88 Sqn despatched an offensive patrol on the 4th, all four Bristols had at least one ace aboard. Conn had Sgt C M Maxwell as his observer when he claimed a Dr I out of control near Provin, while Johnston claimed another, along with two D VIIs, with fellow Aussie Lt Walter Irving Newby Grant, an 18-year-old former bank clerk, as his observer. Lt C Foster's observer, Lt Smyth, also claimed one out of control, while Lt Findlay, with 2Lt C T Gauntlett as his observer, sent one crashing for his eighth victory. Digby-Worsley rejoined Conn to down a Fokker D VII out of control on the 5th, while Hepburn and Eldon accounted for two D VIIs, one in flames. Hepburn and Eldon got another D VII the next day.

On 16 September, Conn and Digby-Worsley attacked a Fokker D VII over Harbourdin aerodome, near Lille, and saw it spin down and collide with another Fokker, both aeroplanes subsequently crashing. On the 20th they sent a Fokker down put of control and shared in the destruction of another with two other Bristol crews – Lt George Ramsden Poole (his fifth and final victory) and Sgt Hill, as well as Capt Johnston and Lt Grant, their sole known victim, Ltn Helmut Gantz of *Jasta* 56, dying of his wounds in hospital the next day.

Johnston and Grant bagged an LVG two-seater on the 22nd, while Hepburn and Eldon destroyed a D VII in flames near Harbourdin on the 24th, killing Vzfw Peter Stenzel of *Jasta* 14. Johnston and 2Lt H R Goss drove a D VII down out of control near Abancourt on the 27th, but Lt C Foster and Thomas Proctor were shot down and killed by Vzfw Fritz Classen of *Jasta* 26.

Johnston and Sgt C M Maxwell downed two D VIIs between Wavrin and Berlaw in 2 October, while Charles Findlay teamed up with Lt Ivan Wilmot Frank Agabeg, a 22-year-old Londoner, to destroy two more near La Bassée. Johnston and Agabeg downed a Fokker near Meruchin the next day, and although their aeroplane was shot-up, they made Allied lines unhurt, while Ken Conn and Lt A B Radford destroyed another D VII. The 4th saw four more successes for the squadron, including a

Scottish-born Capt Charles Findlay was credited with 14 victories in No 88 Sqn – nine with his front gun, the other five downed by his observer – and in spite of his participation in several strafing attacks on enemy aerodromes, never took a bullet in his Bristol. He also took part in experiments in the use of wireless telegraphy between aircraft (*Norman Franks*)

Born in Perth, Western Australia, on 30 April 1896, Capt Edgar Charles Johnston scored his first victory flying a DH 5 with No 24 Sqn, followed by 19 more in Bristols with No 88 Sqn (*Jack Eder*)

shared D VII and a Halberstadt as the fifth and sixth victories for No 88 Sqn's other Findlay, Lt John Pierce Findlay from South Africa, whose observer that day was 2Lt R E Hasell. Charles Findlay and Ivan Agabeg destroyed a Fokker on the 7th, and Hepburn and Eldon added D VIIs to their joint accounts on the 8th and 9th.

Lt Jefferies poses before his F 2B E2220, which is seen in typical livery for 'C' Flight of No 88 Sqn (*Jack Eder*)

During a sizeable scrap on the 23rd, Conn and 2Lt D A Vavasour sent a D VII down to crash, Lt H C Foley got one out of control and 20-year-old Gerald Frank Anderson from Natal, South Africa, drove another down out of control for his sixth of eight victories. The real damage to the enemy, however, was more likely done by the team of Alec Williamson and Walter Grant, who each claimed Fokkers near Beclers, observer Grant's going down in flames. Lt W B Clark, observer to Lt William Allan Wheeler, also claimed a D VII in flames over Leuze. Their victims were probably Vzfws Emil Hanzog and Alfred Nauwerk of *Jasta* 57, killed at Bantigny that day. Hepburn sent a D VII down out of control on the 28th, while Lt Vivian Voss forced another to land.

No less than 14 Fokkers were claimed by No 88 Sqn on 30 October, including two for Conn, two for Charles Findlay and Agabeg (the pilot's 14th victory and the observer's fifth), one for Wheeler (bringing his score to eight) and one to Lt J Baird and Sgt Hill, bringing the latter's total to seven. Another was the seventh credited to Voss' observer, Sgt Antcliffe. The squadron's last air-to-air successes came on 4 November, when Hepburn downed a Pfalz D XII, his Scottish observer, Alexander Tranter, sent another crashing for his seventh victory, Agabeg scored his seventh over a Fokker D VII with Lt L E Lacoste as his pilot, and Conn, with 2Lt K C W Craig as his observer, despatched a Fokker for his 20th.

Conn joined the budding RCAF after the war, but injuries suffered in a crash in 1921 ended his flying career. Rejoining the RCAF in World War 2, he rose to the rank of group captain and became director of staff duties at Air Force Headquarters. After his second world war, Conn resumed his civilian position as general manager of University Tours Ltd in Toronto. He died on 30 January 1984.

Credited with 16 victories and awarded the DFC, Allan Hepburn joined the RAAF in 1921 and became a wing commander in the 1930s. He died on 21 July 1975.

'A' Flight prepares for take-off late in 1918, with Capt Allan Hepburn's F 2B F4442, distinctively marked with a large number '1' and the crest of the Australian Armed Forces, leading the pack at left (*Jack Eder*)

Edgar Johnston also returned to Australia to become its controller of civil aviation from 1933 to 1936, assistant director general of the department of civil aviation from 1939 to 1955 and advisor to Qantas Airlines from 1955 to 1967. After celebrating his 90th birthday in Melbourne in 1986, he died on 22 May 1988.

PUSHING PAST THE PIAVE

Given its performance and versatility, the Bristol F2B's use on Britain's other far-flung battlefronts was limited only by production and Western Front priorities. Once enough were available, Bristols also gave sterling service over Italy and the Middle East as well.

Following the disastrous Italian defeat at Caporetto on 26 October 1917, both France and Britain sent assistance to their beleaguered ally, including squadrons of aircraft. In March 1918 the British contribution included a flight of Bristol F 2Bs, commanded by Capt T C Lowe MC, which was initially attached to Sopwith Camel-equipped No 28 Sqn at Grossa. From there the flight was almost immediately transferred to No 34 Sqn at Istrana, where it was designated 'Z' Flight.

Subsequently based at Villaverla, the flight's Bristols mostly carried out long-range reconnaissance missions, which would have been more hazardous for No 34 Sqn's regular complement of slower RE 8s. F 2B B1212 failed to return from one such sortie on 25 April, and over the next month indications grew of Austro-Hungarian preparations for a new offensive.

It was also clear that the Austro-Hungarian fighter pilots were neither intimidated by the Bristol's fearsome reputation nor adversaries to be taken lightly. On 10 May F 2B C4755 was brought down by Oblt Frank Linke-Crawford of *Fliegerkompagnie* (*Jagd*) 60, or *Flik* 60J, and its crew, Lts J B Guthrie and H Y Thornton, made PoWs. While on a western reconnaissance on 2 June, 2Lts E M Brown and H Milburn attacked five Albatros D IIIs over Borgo and sent one down out of control before being themselves brought down as PoWs. On the 9th, three Bristols spotted six Albatros, and during the fight which ensued, 2Lts A E Ryan and T Newey downed one in flames and Lt G Robertson and 2Lt Milburn claimed another, but Capt Lowe and his observer, 2Lt A S Withers, were wounded and crash landed at Villaverla, victims of Fw Sandor Kasza of *Flik* 55J.

On 15 June the Austro-Hungarians launched their final attempt to force their way across the Piave River, attacking from east of Asiago to the sea. The RAF joined the Italian air arm in bombing and strafing every bridge, raft, boat and troop concentration they could find, with 'Z' Flight playing its part by carrying out constant reconnaissance missions. On the 24th the Austro-Hungarian onslaught was repulsed, with some 20,000 casualties and the loss of many guns.

At the end of the month a second flight of Bristols arrived, and on 3 July, the expanded 'Z' Flight was officially redesignated No 139 Sqn, under the command of Canadian Capt A A Harcourt-Vernon. The new squadron flew its first combat sortie the next day, as two F 2Bs, crewed by

Italian airmen and soldiers assist members of No 139 Sqn in recovering F 2B D8084 after a crash at Villaverla. Originally marked with two white bands and the letter 'T', near the end of the campaign D8084 sported 12 bands, the letter 'S' and a Charlie Chaplin figure on the cowling (*Colin A Owers*)

Lt A L McLaren and 2Lt H Baldwin, and Lt H C Walters and 2Lt G Beagle, flew a 'western recce', escorted by two other Bristols crewed by Lt Walter Carl Simon – an American from New Orleans, who had been with the unit since 'Z' Flight's inception in March – and William Watson Smith, and Lt Wood and AM J C Ings.

The quartet encountered four 'Albatros D IIIs' over Levico aerodrome, and after Walters became separated from the others, his observer, Beagle, fired four bursts into their nearest antagonist and saw it turn over on its back and crash north of Orsola – possibly killing Kpl Franz Pelzmann of *Flik* 55J, who was actually flying a Phönix D II. Simon and Smith then took on another assailant, and after firing three short-range bursts, the latter saw the enemy aircraft go down out of control.

On 11 July Harcourt-Vernon fired 100 rounds of Vickers at ground targets, with his gunner, 2Lt Milburn, adding 120 Lewis rounds to the enemy's misery. Walters and Smith carried out a similar strafing attack two days later.

NEW CO

On 14 July No 139 Sqn got a new commander in the shape of Canadian Maj William George Barker, who had previously scored 38 victories with Nos 28 and 66 Sqns (see *Osprey Aircraft of the Aces 52 – Sopwith Camel Aces of World War 1* for further details). Barker was far from pleased to be assigned a two-seater unit, and although allowed to keep his Camel B6313, he painted a heart with an arrow through it on the vertical stabiliser, telling anyone who asked that it symbolised his own. Barker also painted four white bands on the fuselage of the Sopwith fighter –

double the squadron's usual number – which he subsequently increased to seven later.

Morale at No 139 Sqn was not terribly high when Barker arrived, either. The unescorted reconnaissance missions, which limited the Bristol's capability of mixing it with enemy fighters, had much to do with the three aeroplanes and six men the squadron had lost behind enemy lines between April and June. Barker encouraged a more aggressive policy among his aircrews' approach and set the example, albeit mainly in his Camel. His successes in the next few weeks inspired the 'Biff boys', although Walter Simon seems to have needed little prompting to emulate his CO.

On 15 July four Bristols flew a western reconnaissance, but one had to turn back. The remaining three encountered eight enemy fighters over Mattarello and immediately attacked. Walters and Smith sent one down, smoking badly, to crash at Cortesano. Simon and Ings, along with Lts G W Curtis and Baldwin, fought the other Austro-Hungarians, until Simon got a burst into an Albatros D III and saw it crash at Migzone. In spite of a jammed gun, Curtis and Baldwin scattered the rest of their assailants.

Barker downed two two-seaters on the 18th for the first of eight victories with No 139 Sqn – all scored while flying his beloved Camel. He was, however, flying Bristol D8075, with Smith as his observer, on 16 July when he drove down an Albatros that was not credited to him. After scoring a double victory in his Camel on 20 July, Barker destroyed an Albatros over Godega aerodrome on the 23rd, while Walters and Davies claimed another 'out of control'. On the same day, however, two Bristols on lone patrols to the east were lost, Lt V D Fernald and 2Lt W Watkins being shot down in flames by Oblt Roman Schmidt of *Flik* 30J, while Lt W L Vorster and Sgt H G Frow fell victim to Oblt Friedrich Navratil of *Flik* 3J.

Coincidentally, both of the victors came from Croatia, and each had just scored his fifth victory. Both also saw to it that their respective victims were buried with full military honours.

On 30 July Capt Sydney Dalrymple, an experienced veteran of Nos 27 and 24 Sqns, led a three-aeroplane western reconnaissance with Ings as his observer. At 14,000 ft, Lt Simon, in his usual F 2B C999, spotted two two-seaters and seven Albatros D IIIs 4000 ft below, signalled the others and dived, quickly sending down a D III in flames. Making a right-hand climbing turn, he then downed another fighter in flames with a 100-round burst. Four more fighters attacked his Bristol, wounding Smith, but as he turned, Simon found himself under the two-seaters and Smith, in spite of his wound, fired 70 rounds into one and sent it down to crash between Torri di Mosa and Caorle.

Capt Sydney Dalrymple was one of the few aces to claim a victory while flying a Martinsyde Elephant. The remaining four of his five successes were scored over the Italian front, mostly in F 2B D8084 (*Norman Franks*)

Austro-Hungarian soldiers examine F 2B D7966 of No 139 Sqn, brought down at Gardolo by Oblt Friedrich Navratil of *Fliegerkompagnie* 3J on 23 August 1918. The crew, Lts C E Gill and T Newey, were taken prisoner (*Colin A Owers*)

As the fight descended to 6000 ft, Simon found himself coming head-on at the other two-seater, fired at it at less than 100 yards' distance and saw it go down out of control. At an altitude of 2000 ft, Simon made his way toward Allied lines, while Smith sent another attacking Albatros down out out of control. Simon was subsequently awarded the DFC, but Austro-Hungarian records reveal no losses that correspond to Simon and Smith's 'ace-in-one-mission' exploit.

At about that same time, Barker was asked by Capt William Wedgwood Benn of No 34 Sqn to drop an Italian spy behind Austro-Hungarian lines by parachute from a specially fitted-out Savoia-Pomilio SP 4. The agent, Alessandro Tandura, was successfully dropped on 9 August, and would send valuable information to the Allies right up to the end of the war. Benn also made several local flights in No 139 Sqn's Bristols to drop carrier pigeons and food.

The day before Tandura's drop, 8 August, had seen Dalrymple resume a progress toward acedom that had begun on 1 July 1916, when he downed a Roland C II while flying a Martinsyde G 100 Elephant with No 27 Sqn. Flying with Baldwin, in company with Lts Curtis and Beagle, and Simon with Sgt M Akam in place of the wounded Smith, Dalrymple spotted a lone Albatros high over Trento, and after firing 40 rounds at the fighter, it went spinning down, although it was seen to recover at about 6000 ft.

The British encountered two more Albatros scouts and Dalrymple fired 70 rounds into one, which stalled, passed over his upper wing and burst into flame after Baldwin fired another 70 rounds into it. Dalrymple then downed a second fighter in flames over Caldonazzo. His victims were apparently Phönix D IIs of *Flik* 9J, both pilots, Zugsführer Karl Linner and Fw Johann Pinkalsky, being killed.

Two days later, Simon and Akam spotted two enemy fighters over Caldonazzo, and Simon sent one crashing into a wood, bringing his final tally to eight.

The Canadian commander of No 139 Sqn, Capt William G Barker DSO MC, takes HRH Edward, Prince of Wales, up on an unofficial 'flip' from Villaverla aerodrome in the observer's pit of F 2B D8063 (*Colin A Owers*)

On 16 August Dalrymple led four Bristols on a bombing raid, striking at Levico aerodrome and Primalano, but F 2B D8069 was shot down in flames by Oblt Navratil, and its crew, Lts C R H Jackson and W Keepin, were killed. On the 22nd, Lts N Gwyer and T Hilton were brought down as PoWs, probably becoming the fifth victory for Fw Karl Teichmann of *Flik* 14J. During a scrap between two Bristols and four Albatros D IIIs the next day, 2Lt J B Isaacs' gun jammed, but his observer, Capt M Cahill-Byrne, claimed one of their antagonists out of control and another in flames. Lts C E Gill and T Newey were less fortunate, however, Navratil riddling their engine and forcing them to land near Gardolo to become PoWs.

Reconnaissance and photo sorties continued until 13 September, when Dalrymple led four Bristols west and encountered ten Albatros D IIIs 15,000 ft above Trento. Half-rolling onto one's tail, Dalrymple chased it down to 12,000 ft, fired a close-range burst and set it afire. Another came down on him, but his observer, Beagle, fired three drums of Lewis rounds into it and sent it, too, down in flames. Curtis and Ings also claimed three enemy aeroplanes in the fight, and two other fighters were credited to the teams of Lt H V Jellicoe and Sgt F H Shanks, and Lt Isaacs and 2Lt W Abram.

ROYAL VISITOR

On 16 September No 139 Sqn welcomed a royal visitor in the person of Edward, Prince of Wales, then attached to the staff of Gen Frederick Rudolf Lambart, 10th Earl of Cavan, and commander of British forces in Italy. The prince, who had flown at least once in France, believed the aeroplane to have more potential as a weapon than the tank, and on more than one occasion Barker took him up for 'joy rides' in an F 2B. During one 'flip' Edward's aide, Capt Lord Sir Claud Nigel Hamilton, accompanied him in Simon's Bristol and became violently airsick, much to the prince's amusement!

With Austro-Hungary already out of the war, members of No 139 Sqn pose before one of their Bristols upon learning of the armistice on the Western Front on 11 November 1918. Identified personnel include Lt W Abram (front row, left), and third from left in second row, Capt G W Curtis, Maj H H Kitchener (holding mascot), Capt Walter C Simon, Lt J B Isaacs and 2Lt W T Davies. Others include Lt E Exton (standing third row, second from left), Lt R G Fullager (third row, third from right), Lt H Milburn (back row, second from left) and Lt H V Jellicoe (back row, right) (*Norman Franks*)

On another sortie, whose extraordinary duration worried the staff officers and aides, Barker was believed to have flown up to the line and Prince Edward fired off a couple of Lewis drums at the enemy trenches. Neither Barker nor Edward admitted to have ventured so near harm's way, but the prince's map reading knowledge was noticed to have suspiciously improved after their return. Word of those excursions inevitably reached the ear of King George V, who sternly admonished his son over his risky exploits.

On 30 September, Barker was recalled to England and Dalrymple took temporary charge of No 139 Sqn until its new commander, Maj H H Kitchener – a nephew of the late Lord Herbert Horatio Kitchener – arrived on 23 October.

That month saw an Allied build-up for what would prove to be the final great battle in Italy, during which No 139 Sqn's aeroplanes were carrying 112-lb bombs to attack enemy airfields and installations in addition to photographing the terrain and strafing trenches.

On the 9th, the squadron moved to Grossa, 12 miles northwest of Padua. The Allied assault over the Piave began on the 27th, and within three days the Austro-Hungarian army was in full retreat. The last casualties for No 139 Sqn occurred on 30 October, when Capt L Hursthouse and Lt H Dowse came back wounded, and Isaacs and Cahill-Byrne were brought down by ground fire and taken prisoner.

Moving up to Arcade on 1 November, No 139 Sqn did its part to keep up the pressure until the 4th, when word arrived that the Hapsburg Empire had surrendered.

Disbanded on 7 March 1919, No 139 Sqn had performed 60 long-range reconnaissance missions and 64 offensive patrols, also dropping 5 1/2 tons of bombs and claiming 26 enemy aircraft destroyed and another eight 'out of control'. Walter Simons and William Smith shared eight victories between them, while Sydney Dalrymple's four brought his wartime total to five.

OVER THE HOLY LAND

For all its achievements elsewhere, it was arguably over Palestine that the Bristol F 2B may have played its most significant rôle in establishing Allied air superiority and affecting the overall success of the campaign. This is the more remarkable when one considers that no more than a single squadron of 'Biffs' operated over that theatre of operations.

In August 1917, a fighter flight detached from No 14 Sqn in Palestine, was expanded into No 111 Sqn and equipped with six Bristol F 2Bs. The effect these high performance fighters had in an aerial environment that had hitherto been dominated by the German *Flieger Abteilungen* 300, 301, 302, 303 and Bavarian 304, as well as the provisional *Pascha Jagdstaffel* made up of Albatros D IIIs attached to those units, was not long in revealing itself.

The Bristols' presence was regarded as a godsend by neighbouring No 67 Sqn, whose all-Australian personnel had been making do with a mixed bag of hand-me-down BE 2s, Bristol Scouts, Martinsyde G 100 and G102 Elephants, BE 12s and RE 8s.

'Because our duty was reconnaissance, it was necessary that we spent most of our time in the air behind the Turkish lines, where we were vulnerable to attack by the German Air Service, who had much superior aircraft', recalled the unit's former commander, Air Marshal Sir Richard Williams. 'Until No 111 Sqn obtained the Bristol Fighters in late 1917,

Personnel of No 67 Sqn RFC – including the ubiquitous mascots – jubilantly form up before a line-up of BE 2es, Martinsyde G 100 Elephants and the first of the Bristol F 2Bs transferred over from No 111 Sqn in January 1918. At right, leaning on his cane, is the commander, Capt Richard Williamson (*Australian War Memorial via Colin A Owers*)

Bristols A7194 and B1150 undergo maintenance near a typical hangar used by No 1 Sqn AFC at El Mejdel. Note the camera mounted on A7194 (*Australian War Memorial via Colin A Owers*)

we did not shoot down or capture any enemy airmen, but we did lose many of our own men due to the action of the German air service, anti-aircraft fire, and engine failure.

'By the end of 1917 we were re-equipping with Bristol Fighters, and this was the first time that we were in a position to really stand up and attack our opponents', he continued. 'The Germans soon found out about it, and they kept as far away from the Bristol Fighters as they could. This aircraft was, I consider, the best service aircraft produced in World War 1. It could do any job required to be performed by a pilot and observer, and it could look after itself'.

The Bristol flight made its presence known in earnest on the morning of 8 October 1917, when F 2B A7194, crewed by 2Lt R C Steele and Capt John Jordan Lloyd Williams, a former member of the Denbigh Yeomanry, encountered an Albatros D III and brought it down at Wadi Gaza, where its pilot, Oblt Gustav Adolf Dittmar of *Fl.Abt.* 300, was taken PoW. A week later Steele and Williams destroyed another D III at Shellah-Sharia, killing Ltn d R Richard Ernert of *Fl.Abt.* 301. Capt Arthur Hicks Peck, who had been born in India on 25 April 1889 and educated at Cambridge before wartime led to his joining the RFC, was the pilot of A7194 on 30 October when he and Williams brought down a two-seater northwest of Khalasa, again resulting in the capture of its crew.

These materially modest, but psychologically significant, aerial successes occurred on the eve of the Third Battle of Gaza, in which the British forces, under General Sir Edmund Henry Hynman Allenby, achieved a decisive breakthrough against their Turco-German opponents. During the battle, which occurred between 31 October and 7 November, Peck and Williams again demonstrated the Bristol's ascendancy when they caught a high-speed, high-altitude Rumpler C IV reconnaissance aeroplane on 6 November, forced it to land at Um Dabkel and then destroyed it on the ground. Two days later, the duo sent an Albatros D III down in flames over Kuleikat, the pilot, Oblt Rolf Scheler of *Fl.Abt.* 304b, dying of his wounds on the 13th.

Riding their momentum into southern Palestine, Allenby's troops took Jerusalem on 9 December. On the 12th, Capt Roy Maxwell Drummond and 2AM F J Knowles opened their account in convincing style by

Bristol F 2B A7194 displays the PC 10 and white finish sported by some of the Bristols of No 67 Sqn – later redesignated No 1 Sqn AFC. Prior to transferring to that unit, A7194 had seen considerable success with No 111 Sqn, as flown by pilots 2Lt R C Steele and Capt A H Peck, and observer ace Capt J J L Williams. At some point in its career, A7194's vertical stabiliser was either replaced or repainted with the surface and serial colours reversed (*Australian War Memorial via Colin A Owers*)

sending an Albatros D V down out of control at Tul Keram at 1030 hrs, destroying a second four miles northwest of that location five minutes later and a third at Wadi Auja at 1045 hrs. Their second victim was probably Ltn d R Heinrich Deilman of *Fl.Abt.* 302, who was killed.

Born in Perth, Western Australia, on 2 June 1894, 'Peter' Drummond, as he preferred to be called, had begun his war as a private in the AIF's Medical Corps, before joining the RFC's No 67 Sqn.

On 20 March 1917, he and Capt D W Rutherford were flying BE 2cs, while Lt A W L Ellis and 2Lt Francis Hubert McNamara were in G 100 'Elephants', as each of the four dropped six modified 4.5-in howitzer shells on a construction train at Wadi Hesse.

During the attack, 'Frank' McNamara's fifth bomb exploded prematurely, severely wounding him in the right buttock, and Rutherford's BE was brought down by ground fire. Without hesitation, McNamara landed to pick up Rutherford, but due to his wound he botched the landing and crashed his aeroplane. Setting it on fire, he ran to Rutherford's machine 200 yards away, and while Drummond and 'Les' Ellis strived to keep some nearby Turkish cavalry at bay, McNamara managed to restart the engine and, in spite of a flat tyre, took off and flew himself and Rutherford to the nearest Allied field, 70 miles away. For his unique feat McNamara became the first Australian airman to be awarded the VC.

Drummond himself had earned the MC, and when he transferred to No 111 Sqn he had teamed up with Knowles, a Scot who hailed from Nairn on the Moray Firth. On 14 December Drummond and Knowles downed another Albatros north of Beisan.

Three days later Lt Charles Robert Davidson, a former member of the Highland Light Infantry who had scored his first two victories in Vickers FB 19 Bullets with Nos 14 and 111 Sqns, was flying A7192 with 2Lt A Simmons in the 'back seat' when they engaged a two-seater, killed the observer, *Rittmeister* Karl *Freiherr* von dem Busche-Strethorst of *Fl.Abt.* 302, forced it to land five miles north of Bireh and then destroyed the aeroplane. Davidson and Simmons similarly drove down and strafed a two-seater near Nablus on the 22nd, and Davidson and Knowles repeated that performance in the Nablus valley on the 28th, although on both occasions the German crewmen survived. Davidson and Simmons drove down an Albatros D III out of control on the 29th, bringing the pilot's final tally to six, for which he would be awarded the MC on 14 January 1918, five days after leaving the squadron.

ACE'S DEBUT

Another of No 111 Sqn's aces made his scoring debut on 17 January when Canadian Lt Austin Lloyd Fleming, flying A7192, with Knowles as

At one point in its career, F 2B A7198 had strikingly alternating PC 10 and white wing uppersurfaces, as seen here. At another, the wings were white overall. Personnel shown are, from left to right, Capt Richard Williams, Lt Gen Sir Harry George Chauvel (commander, Desert Mounted Corps), Lt Col Frank Graham Newton (5th Light Horse Regiment, AIF) and Capt W Sydney Addison (*Australian War Memorial via Colin A Owers*)

his observer, destroyed a two-seater at Kalikieh. The same team was in A7198 the next day, sharing in the destruction of another two-seater between Jaffa and Arsuf with Lt D B Aitken and L A J Barbe. Shortly after that, No 111 Sqn was re-equipped with Nieuport and SE 5a single-seat scouts, bequeathing all of its Bristols to No 67 Sqn. Fleming subsequently raised his total to eight and earned the MC flying SE 5as.

Peter Drummond also raised his score to eight in a Nieuport, and continued his career in the RAAF, having reached the rank of Air Marshal by the time he was killed in a air accident in Canada on 27 March 1945.

Peck added five to his previous three Bristol victories flying SE 5as, also earning the DSO, MC and Bar, taking command of No 25 Sqn in 1923, serving in Iraq in 1928 and attaining the rank of group captain in 1935. Of the observers, Knowles received the MM and promotion to corporal in 1918, and was later awarded the MC.

While No 111 Sqn transitioned to single-seaters, No 67 Sqn unleashed its new F 2Bs on 3 January 1918, when 16 of them dropped 1200 lbs of bombs on El Afuleh aerodrome, where *Fl. Abt.* 302 and 304b were based. On the way home two Albatros D IIIs attacked the formation and Lts R A Austin and Leslie W Sutherland, in F 2B B1128, claimed one of them for the squadron's first Bristol victory. On the 23rd Capt W Sydney Addison and Tasmanian-born Lt Wilmot Hudson Fysh, the latter a former 3rd Light Horse Regiment veteran of Gallipoli, claimed an Albatros D V near El Bireh.

A significant event of a different nature followed on 6 February, when No 67 Sqn RFC was redesignated No 1 Squadron AFC, and in March the unit moved up to the newly taken town of El Mejdel.

Meanwhile, the Germans responded to the growing threat posed by the Bristols and SE 5as. Between 15 and 30 March 1918, *Jasta* 55 arrived at Jenin, Palestine, and was redesignated *Jasta* 1F in reference to its affiliation with Marshal Erich von Falkenhayn's *Heeresgruppe* F, commanded since February by Marshal Otto Liman von Sanders.

On 31 March No 1 Sqn AFC achieved its full strength of 18 F 2Bs, and on 2 April two of them reconnoitred the Jenin area to discover a new airfield under construction and 14 new aeroplanes on the ground. The desert sky heated up anew on 15 April as four Bristols were attacked by three Albatros near Tul Kerm, but two German fighters were claimed to have been shot down. On the 28th, four F 2Bs were engaged by four

Capt W Sydney Addison and Lt Wilmot Hudson Fysh prepare to take off on a mission from Mejdel, Palestine. After sharing in downing an Albatros D V with Addison on 23 January 1918, Fysh went on to score four more victories with Lt Paul J McGinness – and continued their team-up after the war, as co-founders of Queensland and Northern Territories Air Service (QANTAS) (*Australian War Memorial via Colin A Owers*)

Albatros D Vs and three driven down, one of whose pilots, Ltn d R Fritz Bötzow of *Jasta* 1F, crashed to his death at Nablus. Among the claimants was 30-year-old Lt Edward Patrick Kenny, from Trafalgar, Victoria, and his observer, Lt F C Hawley, in C4626.

Foremost among the nine pilots who achieved acedom in No 1 Sqn AFC was Ross Macpherson Smith. Born in Adelaide, South Australia, on 4 December 1892, Smith had ridden with the Australian Light Horse before joining No 67 Sqn. While flying BE 12 A6311 on 1 September, he teamed up with Maj 'Les' Ellis to shoot down an Albatros D III over Beersheba, a success confirmed when the British intercepted a German wireless message stating that Ltn Schmarje, a pilot of *Fl. Abt.* 300 with at least two British aircraft to his credit, had crashed but survived.

'Ross Smith came to No 1 Sqn as an observer when we were on the Suez Canal', recalled Sir Richard Williams. 'Apart from the time he spent whilst retraining to become a pilot, he served with the squadron right through the campaign, until its end. He was a very solid, reliable type of man. He always took the keenest interest in his aircraft and men – much more so than the average pilot. I'm sure that this was the foundation of his success with his team on the first England-to-Australia flight. He had served in aircraft inferior to those used by the Germans, and he was really in his element when he came into the possession of a Bristol Fighter'.

Smith scored all the rest of his 11 victories in F 2B B1229. The first, a Rumpler brought down one mile southeast of Jenin on 7 May 1918, was also the first of five scored in concert with Lt Ernest Andrew Mustard. Born in Oakleigh, Victoria, on 21 September 1893, 'Pard' Mustard, who

A superb view of one of No 1 Sqn's Bristols 'stripped naked' for maintenance, showing a wealth of detail of the fuselage structure and the Rolls-Royce Falcon III engine (*Australian War Memorial via Colin A Owers*)

would change his name to 'Mustar' after the war – had worked on the railways and served in the Signal Service, including time with the 29th Australian Battalion at Gallipoli in 1915, before transferring to the AFC in 1917. Also sharing in the kill was Bristol B1276, crewed by Lts Albert Victor Tonkin and R A Camm, their victims, Vzfw Karl Käppeler and Ltn d R Richard Wolff of *Fl.Abt.* 300, dying of their wounds the next day. Tonkin and Camm also drove two Albatros D Vs down out of control 20 minutes later.

The premier team at No 1 Sqn, Capt Ross M Smith and Lt Ernest A Mustard, prepare for take-off, presumably in their usual F 2B B1229 (*Australian War Memorial via Colin A Owers*)

'As soon as the Huns discovered that we were equipped with aircraft that could chase them, they adopted the practice of running away whenever they saw our aircraft', Williams explained. 'It was quite common for the Germans to dive down and land on the nearest piece of suitable ground whenever they were attacked by a Bristol Fighter. On one occasion, when a German pilot did just that, Smith, accompanied by his usual observer, "Pard" Mustar, came down and landed alongside the German machine. Mustar fired a burst from his Lewis into the German machine, puncturing the petrol tank. Then he fired a Very pistol into the escaping petrol and that spelt the doom of that German machine. The crew were left to get home as best they could, and we often wondered whatever happened to them because the Germans were not popular with the Arabs, and they had a long, long way to travel.'

On 16 May Smith performed one of No 1 Sqn's occasional special missions when he flew Col T E Lawrence to El Tafice after the latter had conferred with Gen Allenby on the matter of obtaining protection for his Bedouin guerrillas from the Turkish and German air attacks that had been undermining their morale in recent weeks.

On 22 May Smith downed an Albatros D V north of Nablus with Lt W A Kirk as his observer. Walter Alister Kirk, who was born in Belfast, Northern Ireland, on 6 August 1887, but he had moved to Lismore, New South Wales, some years later. He had risen to the rank of sergeant in the machine gun section of the 2nd Australian Light Horse, only to be reduced to a private and then commissioned as an officer on 18 December 1916. Entering aviation on 5 July 1917, Kirk joined the AFC as an observer in October. His first two victories had been scored with Lt Eustace Slade Headlam as the pilot – two AEG C IVs forced to land and then strafed near Amman.

Also on 22 May, Tonkin, with Lt C S Paul as his observer, destroyed two Albatros scouts near Nablus. At 0700 hrs on the 23rd Lt Carrick Stewart Paul, a 25-year-old New Zealander, and 27-year-old Lt William James Alexander Weir from Leichhardt, New South Wales, who had been a plantation overseer in Fiji before the war, were patrolling in Bristol C4627, along with Lt George Clifton Peters from Adelaide and James H Traill from Bligh, in New South Wales, in C4623, when they came under attack by Albatros D Vs. In the course of the fight the two Bristols claimed an opponent down out of control and a second that force landed 15 minutes later, after which they destroyed it on the ground.

One of their victims was Vzfw Gustav Schniedewind, a veteran of *Fl. Abt.* 29 and *Jasta* 17, who had scored four victories on the Western Front before adding three more with *Jasta* 1F. The wounds he suffered on 23 May put another German ace out of the war, although Schniedewind recovered to serve briefly in *Fl. Abt.*305 before the armistice.

On 11 June Smith and Kirk teamed up with Lts E G C Stooke and L P Kreig to bring down a Rumpler C IV north of Tul Keram, and on 19 June Smith and Kirk accounted for another Rumpler between Jericho and Damie – in both cases the Germans landed and their aircraft were then destroyed on the ground.

Lost in Action

On 26 June No 1 Sqn suffered its first combat loss in two months when Lts Gordon V Oxenham and Lawrence H Smith failed to return from a patrol in A7236. Smith later described what happened;

'Daylight was just breaking, and with the patrol finished, we were going home. The pilot, G Oxenham, and I were a little way behind, and I spotted two German machines. We swung to meet them, going down, then up between them, and put a burst into one. From 10,000 ft, he went straight down, no smoke or anything. Just in case he straightened up at the last minute and went off for home, we followed him down, but he went straight into the turf. We pulled up to meet the other German aeroplane, and we signalled with our Very pistol to the other aeroplane in our patrol, but by the time they came back to help us, it was all over.

'The second German came down to meet us, but he could not hit us, and we could not hit him. Then Gordon Oxenham, my pilot, was shot through the head and I was shot under the eye. We crashed from about

Evidently pleased just to have survived, Lt Lawrence H Smith, holding pipe in centre, poses before the wreck of F 2B A7236 along with Turkish soldiers and what looks like Ltn Victor Häfner, the German pilot who shot him down on 26 June 1918, at lower right. Smith's pilot, Lt Gordon V Oxenham, was less fortunate, dying in the crash. Smith spent the rest of the war relatively comfortably in German, rather than Turkish, hands (*Australian War Memorial via Colin A Owers*)

Born in Murrumbeena, near Melbourne, Lt Leslie William Sutherland scored eight victories with three pilots in No 1 Sqn between 3 January and 28 September 1918 (*Norman Franks*)

1000 ft. When we hit the ground I was not in the cockpit – if I had have been I would have been crushed. I was dangling over the side, and I fell out. We were both strapped in, so I just hung there.'

Oxenham was killed and Smith captured by *Fl. Abt.* 304b, and their aeroplane credited to Ltn Victor Häfner. Oxenham and Smith's two-seater victim had fared better, the pilot surviving the crash, although the observer, Oblt Fritz Berthold, was severely wounded. The Germans judged it better to keep Smith rather than turn him over to the Turks. 'They kept me there at their squadron, and every time the Turks came to claim me, the German captors would shove me down into a hole, and there I would stay, perhaps for two days', he said. 'There was always food, water, and reading material, and then after the Turks would leave I would come up again and we would all go off into Haifa in the buggy – a railway car powered by an aircraft engine'.

Sometimes on their forays to Haifa, the Germans dressed Smith up in one of their uniforms. They also dropped a letter to his squadron via Jerusalem, since Smith would not reveal his own unit's location. He was frequently interrogated, of course, but recalled, 'If they mentioned the name of an officer in my squadron, I simply had to say that I didn't know him'. Smith was impressed by the courage of *Fl. Abt.* 304b's airmen, noting, 'Their machines were not always as good as ours, but still they had a go. The Germans did not like the Turks one bit', he added. 'I think they liked us better'.

The loss of Oxenham and Smith was summarily avenged the next day when No 1 Sqn took on six enemy aeroplanes near Amman, sent two crashing and forced another to land. That brought the squadron's total for May and June 1918 to 15 aeroplanes shot down and 27 damaged, for the loss of one. By July the Australians were finding it hard to entice the Germans to take on more than two Bristols at a time. After vainly waiting for them to accept their challenge over Jenin, they strafed the aerodrome and damaged five aeroplanes on the ground.

During an encounter with seven Albatros between Birah and Nablus on 16 July, they reported that the entire formation descended and landed hurriedly, rather than engage them. *Jasta* 1F put up more of a fight on the 17th, only to suffer its most disastrous day as three of its Albatros D Vs were shot down – Ltn Kurt Krüger was killed at Beit-Dedshan – and another five aeroplanes returned to Jenin too shot up to be fit for further combat, leaving the *Staffel* with only two serviceable fighters. Two of the Albatros lost that day were downed near Wadi el Auja by Smith and Kirk, bringing the latter's score to seven, and earning him the DFC. Kirk later served as a flight lieutenant in the RAAF during World War 2, and died in Orange, New South Wales, on 6 June 1961.

On 22 July, Lts Tonkin and Sutherland drove down a Rumpler C IV of *Fl. Abt.* 301 south of Beit Lid, Ltn d R Hans Meser and Ltn Gustav Adolf Sakowsky becoming PoWs. On the 30th Kenny and Sutherland forced another Rumpler to land at Wadi Auja, after which they shot the observer and destroyed the plane on the ground. *Fl. Abt.* 303 suffered a galling total of four fatalities that day – Vzfw Ernst Buhl, Uffzs Hugo Müller and Leopold Zaus and Ltn Hermann Weger.

By then the British had established complete air superiority over Palestine. *Flieger Abteilungen* 300 and 302 had ceased flying operations and *Fl. Abt.* 301 would do so at the end of the month. A few Albatros D IIIs arrived as replacements, but attrition continued until only three or four pilots remained at the end of August, and the Germans considered dissolving *Jasta* 1F altogether.

The punishment continued on 3 August, as Kenny and Sutherland forced an Albatros two-seater to land northwest of El Afuleh and destroyed it on the ground at 1130 hrs, then drove a second down out of control over Leijun at 1145 hrs. At 1210 hrs the duo teamed up with Lts Paul Joseph McGinness from Framlington, Victoria, and Hudson Fysh to destroy a third Albatros two-seater northeast of El Duba, killing Vfw Johann Sauer and Ltn d R Heinrich Haars of *Fl. Abt.* 301.

Near Kalkilieh on 24 August, McGinness, with Lt H B Fletcher as his observer, downed a Pfalz in flames, and forced another to land and strafed it, one of the team's victims being Ltn d R Kurt Krüger of *Jasta* 1F. McGinnis and Fysh reunited on the 31st to force an LVG C V down in Allied territory in Rantieh and destroy a second east of Kalkilieh. On 14 September the duo joined Lts D R Dowling and E A Mulford in forcing a Rumpler to land three miles east of Jenin, and then finished it on the ground.

This rare photograph shows Lts Lew Potts and James H Traill of No 1 Sqn discussing their reconnaissance flight in front of Bristol F 2B A7194 at El Mejdel aerodrome, Palestine, in February 1918. Traill, from Bligh, New South Wales, later scored six victories as observer to Lt George Clifton Peters, and was awarded the DFC (*Australian War Memorial, via Colin A Owers*)

ONE-SIDED BATTLES

The battles in the spring and summer of 1918 cost the German flying units in Palestine 40 airmen dead and 20 severely wounded or missing. Much of that butcher bill could be attributed to No 1 Sqn AFC, whose crews claimed some 50 enemy aeroplanes. 'I must say that neither as a squadron commander, nor as a wing commander did I keep any sort of score of enemy aircraft shot down, and given to the credit of any individual or particular pilot, or observer', said Williams.

'Of course, these things were reported and adequately recognised through the award of decorations, etc. But unlike a fighter squadron, No 1 Sqn's job was strategic reconnaissance, bombing, photography, and so on. Its job was to go out and get information and bring it back. Normally, our aircrew fought with anyone who interfered with their mission and in those operations, but the securing of the information requested by Army Headquarters was of the greatest importance to us.'

In September No 1 Sqn moved to Ramleh, and sent a detached flight to Haifa, while Allenby planned his final offensive, to be launched on 19 September. 'He was moving his forces on the ground from the Jordan Valley, up the coast of the Mediterranean, and it was extremely important that the Germans should not discover this', Williams explained.

'We set out to see that no enemy aircraft flew over our lines, or into a position from which they could observe what was happening. If perchance the enemy did observe, then our job was to make certain that the enemy didn't get back with that information to his headquarters. And, in actual fact, we did achieve this! For a fortnight before the advance, not one enemy aircraft that could have obtained vital information about the changes in the disposition of our forces ever returned to his own lines with such information. One of the chief complaints made by the Turkish commander for the ensuing defeat was that they had not been informed of any changes made in the disposition of the British forces. In this particular instance, No 1 Sqn was using the Bristol Fighters purely as fighter aeroplanes.'

On 22 September Ross Smith led a flight to the main camp of Lawrence's Bedouin contingent, just in time to receive reports of a DFW C V and three Pfalz D IIIas approaching. Smith and Mustard took off to intercept in B1229, joined by Lts Headlam and W H Lilly in B1286. After a short fight, the German scouts retired, leaving Smith to dispose of the DFW at Mafrak, east of the enemy airfield at Deraa, at 1000 hrs. The Pfalz came back 45 minutes later, so the Australians sallied up again, Smith forcing one to land near Mafrak, and sharing a second with Headlam, after which they strafed both to destruction. At 1700 hrs another DFW bombed Um Es Surab, drawing Peters and Traill up, along with Lts J M Walker and H A Letch, who drove it down eight miles north of Deraa and then finished it on the ground. That brought Peters' total score up to seven and Traill's to six.

The next morning Kenny and 2Lt Maughan took off from Ramleh and dropped 16 bombs on the hangar at Deraa, setting it on fire, and strafing a line of DFWs on the field. Meanwhile, Allenby had smashed through Turkish lines and No1 Sqn was also engaged in bombing and strafing enemy transport and soldiers as they fled along the Jordan Road toward Wadi Beidan. By the end of what came to be known as the Third Battle of Megiddo, the squadron had expended three tons of bombs and 24,000 rounds of ammunition.

Enemy in Retreat

By 24 September the area west of Amman had been cleared of enemy troops and the Turkish Seventh and Eighth Armies ceased to exist as viable fighting forces. On the 27th the Australians flew over Damascus, strafing the aerodrome there. After a follow-up reconnaissance the next day, Capt Brown reported that the enemy had evacuated the still-burning airfield. The Turks abandoned the city on the 30th.

With the Turks in full retreat, on 19 October Smith and Headlam downed a lone DFW for the squadron's final aerial victory. On the last day of the month, Turkey surrendered. Since 1916, No 67 Sqn RFC/No 1 Sqn AFC had lost 21 men killed in action, 23 wounded and 12 taken prisoner, all of the latter being repatriated.

An F 2B of No 1 Sqn, photographed patrolling at 8000 ft at 0700 hrs on 24 August 1918, embodies the degree of aerial ascendancy that British forces had acquired over Palestine by that time (*Australian War Memorial via Colin A Owers*)

Aside from producing eight aces and Australia's first air VC, several of No 1 Sqn's pilots went on to greater things postwar. Ross Smith and his brother Keith made history – and earned knighthoods – when they left Hounslow in a Vickers Vimy on 19 November 1919 and flew it to Darwin, in Australia, on 10 December. On 14 April 1922, however, Ross Smith was killed in a flying accident.

'Ginty' McGinness (seven victories) and Hudson Fysh (five) were both awarded the DFC and continued their partnership as co-founders of Queensland and Northern Territory Aerial Services, which evolved into Australia's premier international airline, QANTAS. McGinness died on 25 January 1955. Fysh became a Knight of the British Empire and later an author in Sydney, before his death on 6 April 1974.

In addition to Smith, Fysh, Williams and Drummond, a fifth pilot of No 1 Sqn AFC, Lawrence James Wackett, would be knighted for his achievements as founder and managing director of the Commonwealth Aircraft Corporation. Few other flying squadrons could claim to have made so much of a contribution, both during and after the war.

The Bristol Fighter in its various marks remained in production until September 1918, ten months after the armistice, with a total of 4747 being built. In addition to the 13 squadrons that used it over the Western Front, Italy and Palestine, it equipped five Home Defence squadrons, guarding England by night against German airships and bombers.

Poland and Belgium used F 2Bs in the immediate postwar years, and examples would subsequently see service across the globe in the air arms of Spain, Mexico, Eire, Norway, Greece, Canada, New Zealand and the Republic of China.

Of 3830 aircraft on RAF strength as of December 1921, 1090 were Bristol Fighters! Although soon eclipsed as first-line fighters, modified F 2Bs soldiered on in the reconnaissance and bombing rôles over imperial trouble spots in the Middle East and the North West Frontier of India well into the 1920s. A number of surplus airframes were also modified into two-place trainers, serving in the Oxford and Cambridge University Training squadrons until 1931.

For two decades after World War 1, the F 2B's fighting reputation influenced succeeding generations of two-place general purpose fighters, from the Hawker Hart to the Messerschmitt Bf 110, until 1940, when the concept was overtaken by high-performance single-seat fighters in the Battle of Britain. On the other hand, the emergence of supersonic jet fighters equipped with a complex package of radar, guided missiles and other electronic hardware in the second half of the 20th century suggests that the two-seat fighter concept embodied in the Bristol's F 2A/B, given an appropriate update in the back-seater's tasks, may not be so defunct after all.

APPENDICES

Bristol F 2A and F 2B Pilot and Observer Aces

Pilots	Squadron(s)	Score in Bristols	Total	Aircraft Serial(s)
C H Arnison	62	9	9	A4859
A C Atkey	18/22	29	38	B1253
B E Baker	48	12	12	A7170
D W Beard	4/11	7	8	C4846
Wilfred Beaver	20	19	19	?
H H Beddow	22	10	10	D7998
R G Bennett	20	9	9	C4641
J A W Binnie	48	9	9	A7220
N S Boulton	20	6	6	E2213
E C Bromley	22	12	12	C4747/C961
G W Bulmer	22	10	10	C4888
J C Bush	22	6	6	A7174
Lynn Campbell	62	7	7	?
L H T Capel	20	7	7	C4604
J S Chick	11	16	16	C4847
C M Clement	22	6	14	A7172
R D Coath	48/11	8	8	A7174
J H Colbert	20	6	6	B1168
E S Coler	11	16	16	D7912/E2215
Thomas Colvill -Jones	20/48	11	11	B1122
R D Coath	48/11	8	8	A7164/A7213
K B Conn	88	20	20	E2216
D G Cooke	20	13	13	D4749
R J Cullen	88	5	5	D8062
F J Cunninghame	48	5	5	E2507
R L Curtis	48	15	15	A7224
Sydney Dalrymple	139	4	5	A8084
C A Davidson	111	6	4	A7192
H F Davison	22	11	11	B1152/A7243
R E Dodds	48	6	6	?
J E Drummond	48	6	6	?
H W Elliott	48	5	5	A7131
E J Elton	22	16	16	B1152/B1162
J P Findlay	88	6	6	E2474
F G Gibbons	22	14	14	E2454
G E Gibbons	20/62	17	17	E2457
V E Groom	20	8	8	D7939
J E Gurdon	22	28	28	B1162/C989
F G Harlock	20	8	8	?
H H Hartley	48	7	7	A7114
W F J Harvey	22	26	26	E2466
H A Hay	11	5	5	?
Allan Hepburn	88	16	16	C821
F P Holliday	48	17	17	A7108
G H Hooper	11/20	11	11	E2536
G F Hughes	62	11	11	C4630
C E Hurst	22	5	5	C1035
A T Iaccaci	20	17	17	C892/E2213
P T Iaccaci	20	17	17	B1122/E2470
Frank Johnson	22/20/62	12	16	A7144
E C Johnston	88	20	20	E2458
L W King	22	9	7	?
R B Kirkman	20	8	8	B1156
H P Lale	20	23	23	E2467/E2407
Dennis Latimer	20	28	28	C856/C987/ D7993
J H T Letts	27/48/64/87	13	13	A7106
Ernest Lindup	20	5	5	?
R H Little	48	5	5	C841/C814
H G E Luchford	20	13	24	B1122
R M Makepeace	20/11	9	17	?
P S Manley	62	5	5	?
T W Martin	22	6	6	D7896
R F S Maudit	11	9	9	?
Malcolm McCall	20	6	6	?
P J McGinness	1 AFC	7	7	C4623
D M McGoun	20/22	9	9	C4828
A E McKeever	11	30	30	A7144/A7159
T P Middleton	48/20	27	27	C4699/C951
N M Millman	48	6	6	B1190
J T Milne	48	9	9	A7216
E T Morrow	62	7	7	?
W J Mostyn	22	5	5	C901
H C M Nangle	62	5	5	B1245
C G D Napier	20/48	9	9	?
T H Newsome	22	5	5	?
S A Oades	22	11	11	B1152
Keith R Park	48	20	20	C883
C S Paul	1 AFC	11	11	A7182
L A Payne	48	7	7	?
G C Peters	1 AFC	5	5	B1278
G R Poole	88	5	5	?
H J Pratt	48	5	5	?
W T Price	48	7	7	?
T L Purdom	15/62	13	13	B1216
T G Rae	48	6	6	?
G E Randall	20	11	11	E2429
F C Ransley	48	9	9	C768
Richard Raymond -Barker	6/16/48/11/3	6	6	A7112
C R Richards	20	12	12	A6468

Pilots	Squadron(s)	Score in Bristols	Total	Aircraft Serial(s)
A G Riley	48	5	5	?
Norman Roberts	48	7	7	?
D A Savage	62	7	7	B1234
Harry Scandrett	25/11	6	7	A7231
O J F Scholte	18/51/48/60	6	8	?
J P Seabrook	60/8/11	5	5	?
H W Sellars	25/11	8	8	C4673
W C Simon	139	8	8	C999/D8075
D E Smith	20	6	6	?
R M Smith	1 AFC	10	11	B1229
C R Smythe	11	7	7	?
S C Stanton	22	7	7	?
W E Staton	62	26	26	C4619
I A Stead	22	5	5	?
C R Steele	48	7	7	?
T F Stephenson	11	5	5	?
R N M Stuart-Wortley	22/44/88	6	6	?
W K Swayze	62	6	6	C4633
C W K Thompson	22	12	12	C1035
S F H Thompson	20/22	30	30	B1213/C929/E2477
W M Thomson	20	26	26	C843/E2514
A V Tonkin	1AFC	6	6	B1576
T C Traill	20	8	8	?
S H Wallage	22	10	10	C795
F G C Weare	22	15	15	B1253
D J Weston	20	13	13	B1307
W G Westwood	88	6	6	D7942
W A Wheeler	88	6	6	E2458
A M Wilkinson	24/48/23	9	19	?
E G H Williams	48	5	5	?
Alec Williamson	88	9	9	?
W O B Winkler	48	6	6	A3348

Observers	Squadron(s)	Score in Bristols	Total	Aircraft Serial(s)
I W F Agabeg	88	6	6	E2412
C J Agelasto	20	8	9	B883
L W Allen	48	10	10	?
A E Ansell	48	5	5	?
Ernest Antcliffe	88	7	7	C821
T W Barnes	11	9	9	D7978
Walter Beales	48	9	9	C4707
W J Benger	20	5	5	?
M A Benjamin	48	8	8	?
T J Birmingham	22	7	7	D7908
C G Boothroyd	20	12	12	E2407
G A Brooke	45/20	2	7	?
J B Norton	62	5	5	C4709
S W Bunting	22	7	7	B1152
L W Burbidge	20	6	6	?
W C Cambray	20	1	6	A7428
P V G Chambers	62	12	12	B1216
T S Chiltern	88	6	6	E2451
Hugh Claye	62	11	11	C4630
V St B Collins	48/22	10	10	?
A C Cooper	48	7	7	B1190
Roland Critchley	22	7	7	B1162
H G Crowe	20	8	8	C4749
C W Davies	48	5	5	?
L C Davies	22/105	1	5	A7174
E A Deighton	20	15	15	C889/C4604
Brice Digby -Worsley	88	16	16	C4061/E2216
Percy Douglas	11	8	8	C4847
A S Draisey	20	7	7	?
H E Easton	20	8	8	B1156
H L Edwards	20	21	21	E2536
H G Eldon	88	5	5	C821
Thomas Elliott	62	11	11	E2457
Garfield Finlay	1 AFC	7	8	B1149
R M Fletcher	22	26	26	C929/E2477
W H Fysh	1 AFC	5	5	C4623
C J Gass	22	39	39	B1253/E2454
E C Gilroy	11	7	7	C4845/C797
C W Gladman	11	8	8	C972/D7912
Frank Godfrey	20	12	12	C4699/C951
J R Gordon	62	15	15	C4619/C874
Richard Gordon -Bennett	20	5	5	E2252
W I N Grant	88	7	7	C4867
H B Griffith	20/11/48	5	5	A3325
J H Hall	22	5	5	D7896
Ernest Hardcastle	20	12	12	D4764/D7939
G S L Hayward	22	24	24	B1162/B1253
J H Hedley	20	11	11	A7144
R S Herring	48	5	5	?
Charles Hill	88	7	7	?
R F Hill	20	6	7	B1122

Observers	Squadron(s)	Score in Bristols	Total	Aircraft Serial(s)
John Hills	20	7	7	?
G F Hines	62	5	5	?
Edward Hoare	88	7	7	C4720
William Hodgkinson	62	5	5	?
W N Holmes	62	8	8	?
H C Hunt	22	8	8	?
B Jackman	48	6	6	A7170
Frank Johnson	22/20/62	12	16	A7144
J H Jones	22	14	15	C901
P G Jones	20	5	5	?
G H Kemp	20	12	12	C843
W A Kirk	1 AFC	7	7	B1299
S A W Knights	62	8	8	C919
F J Knowles	111	7	7	A7202
G V Learmond	20	9	9	E2429
A D Light	48	8	8	?
H Lindfield	48	6	6	?
Reginald Lowe	62	5	5	E2182
S H P Masding	20	5	5	?
Jack Mason	11	5	5	A7124
M B Mather	20	8	8	B883
G McCormack	22	5	5	?
James McDonald	22	8	8	?
L H McRobert	11	6	6	A7124
A W Merchant	48	8	8	?
H E Merritt	62	9	9	?
Alfred Mills	20	15	15	E2470
L E Mitchell	62	8	8	D7899
E S Moore	48	7	7	A3348
H F Moore	22	6	6	A7286
J L Morgan	22	12	12	B1152
E A Mustard	1 AFC	5	5	B1229
Arthur Newland	20	22	22	D7993/E2213
Walter Noble	20	12	12	B1177/B1307
T C Noel	20	24	24	C856/C987
A R H Noss	48	9	9	A7182
William O'Toole	48	8	8	A7216
Hugh Owen	48	7	7	A7217
Samuel Parry	62	9	9	C4859
S H Platel	11	5	5	?
F A Potter	20	7	7	A6415
L A Powell	11	19	19	A7159
Thomas Procter	88	5	5	?
W C Purvis	45/20	2	5	?
F J Ralph	20	13	13	E2467
V Reed	48	9	9	A7220
J A Richardson	48	5	5	A7114
C C Robson	11	8	8	C4673
John Rudkin	88	10	10	C4867/E2458
J J Scaramanga	20/22	12	12	C989
C J Shannon	22	5	5	?
W W Smith	139	8	8	C999
B H Smyth	88	8	8	E2153

Observers	Squadron(s)	Score in Bristols	Total	Aircraft Serial(s)
L W Sutherland	1 AFC	8	8	C4626
L M Thompson	62	9	9	B1234/C895
George Thomson	22	14	14	C795
A J H Thornton	22	5	5	?
William Tinsley	88	7	7	D7942
C J Tolman	22	8	8	D8089
J H Traill	1 AFC	6	6	B1278
Alexander Tranter	88	7	7	E2339
T C S Tuffield	48	6	6	A7222
R W Turner	20	9	9	?
W U Tyrrell	22	6	6	?
J H Umney	22	13	13	C4747/C961
D P F Uniacke	48	13	13	A7224
M W Waddington	20	5	12	A7255
D E Waight	22	12	12	E2466
William Walker	48	5	5	?
A H W Wall	48	16	16	A7108
E H Ward	88	5	5	D8062
W J A Weir	1 AFC	6	6	C4627
V R S White	45/20	5	6	B1138
J J L Williams	111	5	5	A7194
P S Williams	22	7	7	C4888
A E Woodbridge	20	3	7	?

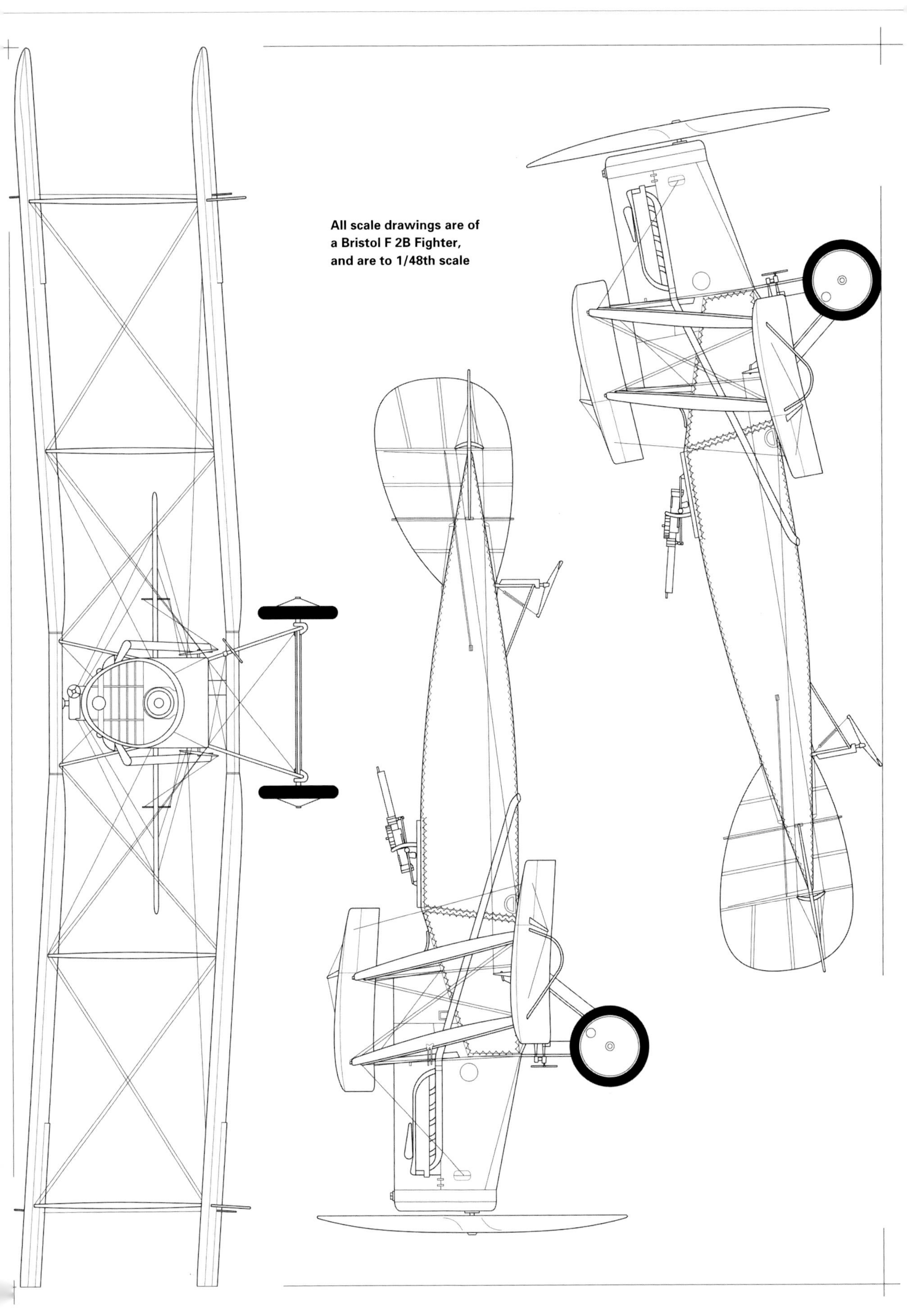

All scale drawings are of a Bristol F 2B Fighter, and are to 1/48th scale

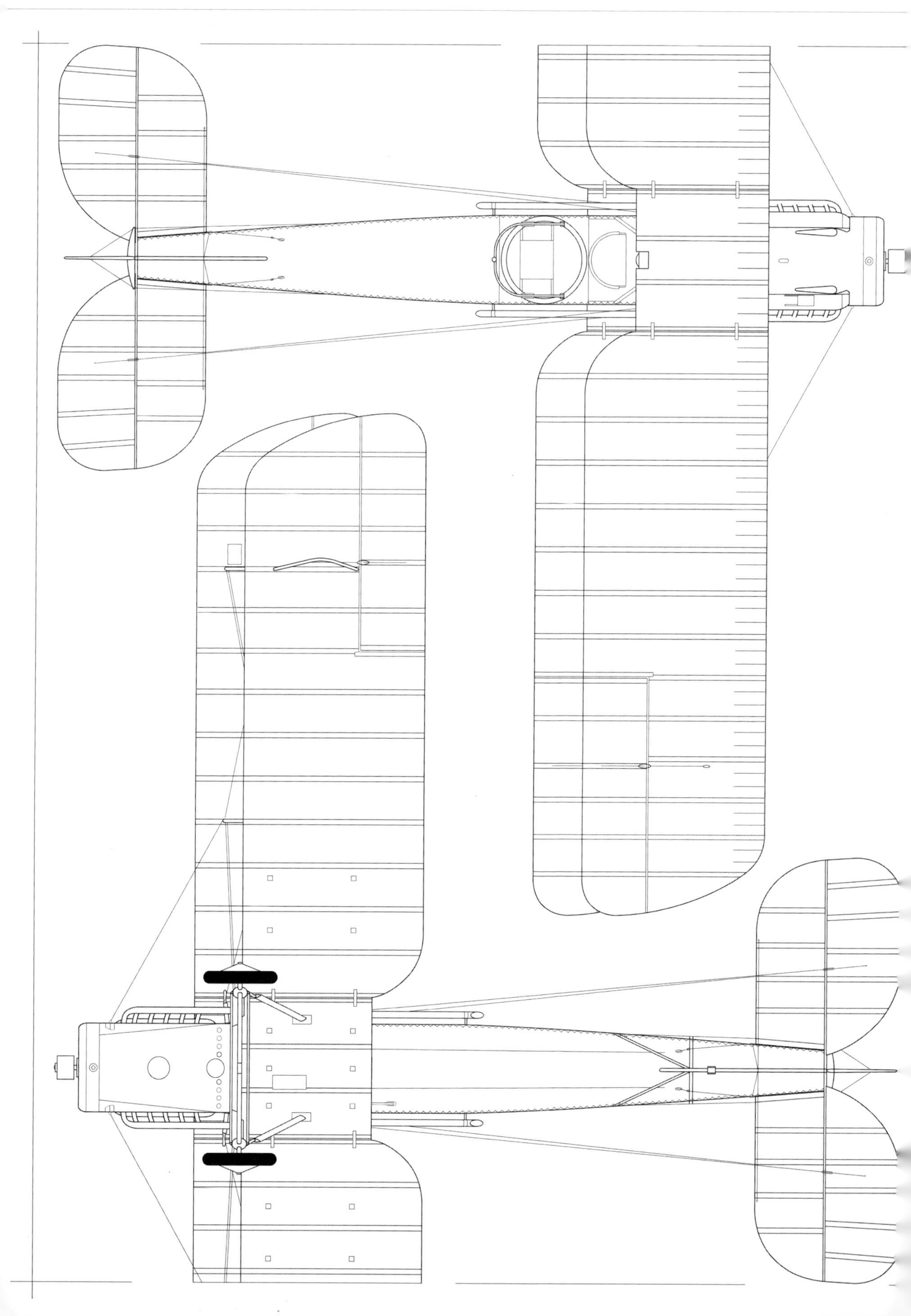

COLOUR PLATES

Artist Harry Dempsey has created the colour profiles for this volume, working closely with the author to portray the aircraft as accurately as circumstances permit. Some of the illustrations are, admittedly, reconstructions based on fragmentary photographic evidence or descriptions provided by the pilots while they were alive, combined with known unit marking policy.

1

F 2A A3325 of Lt Thomas P Middleton and 2Lt Charles G Claye, No 48 Sqn, Bellevue, May 1917

Flying A3325 in Capt William Leefe-Robinson's flight on the disastrous patrol of 5 April 1917, Lts P Pike and Hugh B Griffith managed to survive their run-in with *Jasta* 11, returning to base with credit for an Albatros D III out of control over Douai at 1015 hrs – such a loss is not corroborated by *Jasta* 11 records, however. A3325 probably bore the number '4' on its fuselage by 2 May, when Lts Middleton and Claye, who had previously claimed an Albatros D III on 30 April, used it to down an Albatros two-seater out of control east of Adinfer Wood. After scoring his seventh victory on 18 June, Middleton went home to England for rest, returning in April 1918 as a flight leader in No 20 Sqn. There, he raised his tally to 27, ten of which were scored in F 2B C951. Middleton was awarded the DFC, as were two of his observers, Capt Frank Godfrey (12 victories) and Lt Alfred Mills (15).

2

F 2B A7127 of 2Lts Colin G O MacAndrew and A M West, No 11 Sqn, Fére-en-Tardenois, June 1917

A former member of the Ayrshire Yeomanry Territorial Force, Colin MacAndrew scored his first successes with No 11 Sqn on 28 June 1917, when he and 2Lt A M West claimed two Albatros D Vs over Fresnes. MacAndrew scored another double over D Vs with Lt H C McKenney in the rear cockpit on 9 August, and his fifth on 18 August with Pvte Long as his observer. Posted to fly DH 4s with No 57 Sqn, MacAndrew was killed on 2 October 1917 when his and two other bombers were shot down by pilots of *Jasta* 18. A7127 was later shot down by *Flak Batterie* 102, and photographed in German hands.

3

F 2B A7288 of Capt Andrew E McKeever and 2Lt Leslie A Powell, No 11 Sqn, Fére-en-Tardenois, November 1917

Capt Andrew Edward McKeever scored his last victories in this aeroplane, starting with a DFW C V over Brebières with Lt L V Pogson as his observer. On 30 November, he and 2Lt L F Powell were credited with sending down four Albatros D Vs south of Cambrai, raising McKeever's official tally up to 31 and Powell's to 19.

4

F 2B C4846 of 2Lt Donald W Beard and Sgt H W Scarnell, No 11 Sqn, Plessis-Belleville, March 1918

Born at Sandbach, in Cheshire, on 20 May 1895, Donald Wainwright Beard joined the RFC on 20 August 1913 as an air mechanic. While serving in No 4 Sqn, he got a chance to fly as observer on 20 July 1916, during which flight his BE 2c was attacked and his pilot, Capt Copeland, wounded, although Beard shot down the attacking Pfalz E I and managed to fly the aeroplane back to safety. Following such an extraordinary display of bravery, he was awarded the Military Medal and allowed to train as a pilot, joining No 11 Sqn as a sergeant on 26 November 1917. While flying C4846, with Sgt H W Scarnell as his observer, the newly commissioned 2Lt Beard drove a Pfalz D III down out of control on 9 March 1918, followed by three Albatros D Vs on the 15th. On 22 March, with 2Lt H M Stewart in the back, he destroyed an Albatros D V in flames over Quéant. Two Pfalz D IIIs, downed on 9 June 1918 with Sgt V H Davis as his observer in F 2B C807, brought Donald Beard's overall victory tally to eight.

5

F 2B A7214 of Lts Reginald M Makepeace and Melville W Waddington, No 20 Sqn, Marie Capelle, September 1917

With the arrival of F 2Bs to replace its FE 2ds, No 20 Sqn adopted two vertical white bars on either side of the fuselage roundel as its first unit marking on 26 August 1917. On 3 September, Liverpool-born Canadian Reginald Makepeace and Melville Wells Waddington from Toronto scored the squadron's first Bristol victory when they downed an Albatros D V in flames between Menin and Werwicq in A7214. The pair were flying it again on the 11th when they drove another D V down out of control. Nine of Makepeace's 17 victories were gained in Bristols – one whilst serving as observer to 2Lt John S Chick of No 11 Sqn. Having survived combat on the Western Front, Makepeace perished in a flying accident at Turnberry on 28 May 1918. Waddington's final total came to 12, with five claimed in Bristols.

6

F 2B B1138 of Lts Harry G E Luchford and Victor R S White, No 20 Sqn, Marie Capelle, October 1917

On 5 October 1917, No 20 Sqn began painting over the white bar aft of the fuselage roundel. Lts Harry Luchford and Victor White flew B1138 in that form when they destroyed an Albatros D V on 17 October, a D V and a DFW C V on the 18th and an LVG C V on the 21st, bringing Luchford's total to 24 (11 in FE 2ds and 13 in Bristols) and White's to six. On 2 December Luchford was shot down and killed in F 2B A7292 by Ltn Walter von Bülow of *Jasta* 36, his observer, Capt J E Johnston, surviving as a PoW.

7

F 2B B1307 of Lts David J Weston and Walter Noble, No 20 Sqn, Boisdinghem, June 1918

David John Weston scored 13 victories with No 20 Sqn, six of which were with 37-year-old Walter Noble, who was born in Stowmarket, Suffolk, but who had been a tea-planter in India from 1911 to 1915. Their most notable combat occurred while flying B1307 on 30 June 1918, when they destroyed a Pfalz D IIIa and drove two others down out of control. Both men were awarded the DFC, and Noble, who survived the war with 12 victories, published a memoir, *With a Bristol Fighter Squadron*, in 1920.

8

F 2B D7939 of Lt Victor E Groom and 2Lt Ernest Hardcastle, No 20 Sqn, Boisdinghem, July 1918

Lts Victor Groom and Ernest Hardcastle scored their final two victories – two Fokker D VIIs in flames near Bailleul – on 30 July 1918. On 15 September D7939 was brought down by anti-aircraft fire, and its crew, 2Lt A R D Campbell and Sgt T A Stack, captured.

9

F 2B A7300 of Lts Sydney A Oades and D N G Brampton, No 22 Sqn, Villeneuve-des-Vertus, January 1918

Bearing the three white bands of No 22 Sqn and the legend *PRESENTED BY THE MAHARAJAH OF BAHADUR SIR RAMSEWAR SINGH OF DARBHANGA NO.4*, A7300 was used by Oades and Brampton to drive an Albatros D V down out of control north of Roulers on 6 January 1918 for Oades' fourth victory. A former sapper with the Royal Engineers, Oades had joined the RFC in July 1917 (backdated to 15 May), and after being sent to No 22 Sqn, he scored his first victory over a Rumpler two-seater north of Roulers on 27 October with 2Lt H V R Hill in the observer's pit. Oades claimed two more two-seaters destroyed on 5 and 6 December. A7300 was stricken from No 22 Sqn's rolls on 12 March 1918.

10

F 2B C4810 of Capt George W Bulmer and 2Lt Percy S Williams, No 22 Sqn, Villeneuve-des-Vertus, March 1918

Born in Dixon, Illinois, of British parents on 1 September 1898, Bulmer later settled in Canada. Serving in No 22 Sqn, he scored his first victory – a Pfalz D III out of control east of La Bassée – while flying F 2B C4810 with 2Lt S J Hunter as his observer on 6 March 1918. Ten days later, with Williams in the rear pit, he downed two more Pfalz D IIIs over Henin Lietard. By July Bulmer was a flight leader with at least ten victories, as well as the DFC and MC.

11

F 2B B1152 of Lt Sydney A Oades and 2Lt Stanton W Bunting, No 22 Sqn, Villeneuve-des-Vertus, February 1918

Sydney Oades flew B1152, with S W Bunting as his observer, throughout February 1918, during which time the team sent a two-seater down out of control on 30 January, destroyed an Albatros D V on 17 February, downed another out of control the next day and claimed two more D Vs – including one in flames over Douai – on 26 February. A two-seater and a scout over Lens on 5 March while flying B1168 brought Oades' total to 11, but an injury in a crash on 13 March put him out of the war. B1152 carried on, however, with Lt Hiram Frank Davison and 2Lt J L Morgan using it to down an Albatros on 6 March and three enemy scouts 48 hours later. Flying other Bristols, the pair brought their total to 11 on 29 March, but Davison was wounded on 13 April. Meanwhile, Sgt Ernest J Elton and 2Lt G S L Hayward flew B1152 to down two D Vs on 11 March 1918.

12

F 2B B1162 of Sgt Ernest J Elton and Lt Roland Critchley, No 22 Sqn, Villeneuve-des-Vertus, March 1918

Shown after 22 March, when all squadron markings were removed and the aircraft's personal letters enlarged, B1162 had been Elton's regular aeroplane since the beginning of the month. An air mechanic in No 6 Sqn, Elton had helped to design and construct the gun mounting on Capt Lanoe G Hawker's Bristol Scout in 1915, and was undoubtedly inspired by the ace and VC recipient to put in his application for pilot training, which he subsequently got. Posted to No 22 Sqn, he and his gunner, Sgt John Charles Hagan, downed Albatros D Vs east of Lens on 26 February 1918, before being shot down themselves, but both survived. Switching to B1162, which he up-armed with an overwing Lewis mounting and double guns for his observer, Elton scored another double on 6 March in concert with 2Lt G S L Hayward, destroyed an Albatros on the 8th (with Sgt S Belding) and was flying B1152 on the 11th when he added two more to his tally. Back in B1162 on the 13th, Elton downed two more enemy aeroplanes, then teamed up with Critchley to destroy two D Vs on the 16th, another on the 18th, a Pfalz D III on 26 March and three two-seaters on the 29th. The most successful non-commissioned fighter pilot in the RFC, Elton was awarded the DSM and MM, as well as the Italian *Medaglia di Bronzo al Valore Militare*.

13

F 2B E2466 of Capts W F J Harvey and Dennis E Waight, No 22 Sqn, Agincourt, July 1918

Jim Harvey devised the sturdy overwing Lewis mounting to increase his forward firepower. Although it was easy to change ammunition drums, all that metal affected the compass on the trailing edge of the centre section, and Harvey discarded the device after just one flight. He scored the last nine of his 26 credited victories while flying E2466 between 8 and 22 August 1918, with Capt Dennis E Waight as his observer. Awarded the RAF's very first DFC and a subsequent Bar, Harvey became a farmer after the war, served again in World War 2 and, after retiring in Kent, wrote articles for the aviation magazine *Air Pictorial*, a history of No 22 Sqn (titled *Pi in the Sky*) and became president of the British Cross & Cockade Society from 1969 until his death on 21 July 1972.

14

F 2B A7107 of Lt Ralph L Curtis and 2Lt Desmond P F Uniacke, No 48 Sqn, Bellevue, July 1917

One of the early F 2Bs to arrive at No 48 Sqn, A7107 was crewed by Lt Ralph Luxmore Curtis and 2Lt Laurence W Allen when they destroyed an Albatros D III for Curtis' first and Allen's tenth, and final, victory on 16 June 1917. Curtis flew it again with his usual observer, 2Lt Desmond P F Uniacke, when they destroyed an Albatros D V over Vitry on 7 July. On 21 July Lt Brian E Baker and 2Lt G R Spencer shared in driving down a D V out of contol over Slype for the second of Baker's dozen credited victories. Curtis had brought his score to 15 and Uniacke to 13 when they were shot down and wounded in F 2B A7224 on 21 September by Oblt Hermann Göring of *Jasta* 27, Curtis dying of his wounds and Uniacke becoming a PoW.